# ROUTLEDGE LIBRARY EDITIONS: SOCIOLOGY OF EDUCATION

Volume 18

# CULTURE AND THE GRAMMAR SCHOOL

# CULTURE AND THE GRAMMAR SCHOOL

## HARRY DAVIES

R Routledge
Taylor & Francis Group

LONDON AND NEW YORK

First published in 1965 by Routledge & Kegan Paul Ltd.

This edition first published in 2017
by Routledge
2 Park Square, Milton Park, Abingdon, Oxon OX14 4RN

and by Routledge
711 Third Avenue, New York, NY 10017

*Routledge is an imprint of the Taylor & Francis Group, an informa
business*

*British Library Cataloguing in Publication Data*
A catalogue record for this book is available from the British Library

ISBN: 978-0-415-78834-2 (Set)
ISBN: 978-1-315-20949-4 (Set) (ebk)
ISBN: 978-1-138-22111-6 (Volume 18) (hbk)
ISBN: 978-1-138-22115-4 (Volume 18) (pbk)
ISBN: 978-1-315-41113-2 (Volume 18) (ebk)

**Publisher's Note**
The publisher has gone to great lengths to ensure the quality of this
reprint but points out that some imperfections in the original copies
may be apparent.

**Disclaimer**
The publisher has made every effort to trace copyright holders and
would welcome correspondence from those they have been unable to
trace.

# CULTURE

## and

# THE GRAMMAR SCHOOL

*by*

HARRY DAVIES

LONDON
ROUTLEDGE & KEGAN PAUL

*First published 1965*
*by Routledge & Kegan Paul Ltd.*
*Broadway House, 68-74 Carter Lane*
*London, E.C.4*

To many boys and masters of
High Pavement School
past and present

# CONTENTS

# INTRODUCTION

THE GRAMMAR SCHOOL is under strong attack. Many of its enemies look forward to its early disappearance. Its connection with selection leaves it open to the criticism that it is undemocratic, and that its continued existence causes, or is at least responsible for perpetuating, a gulf in society between the privileged and the unprivileged. Its standards and attitudes are alleged to be those of the middle class, and there are those who say that it would be unable, even if it were willing, to provide for the education of children from working-class homes. It is stated also that its curriculum is excessively academic and is remote both from the interests and the needs of children in the second half of the twentieth century.

In spite of all these criticisms it is my view that the grammar school not only will but should survive: that it stands for important values which our society badly needs, and that it has shown already that it is well able to accommodate children who come to it, in ever-increasing numbers, from under-educated homes. Not, indeed, that all grammar schools are alike. They vary from the large, highly selective middle-class school of the residential area to the small country school, which has been creamed of its social top but includes, otherwise, a fair cross-section of society. They include Smoketown Grammar School, with its large element of urban working-class children, and Manchester Grammar School, with those well-known characteristics which need not be described. In spite of these differences, however, these schools have at least one function in common: they must hand on to a new generation, no matter what its social origin may be, the cultural inheritance without which no man may claim to be properly educated. The success of the grammar school, in contriving to do this for at least the majority of its pupils, is a strong reason why its continued existence is necessary to society.

The grammar school, not unlike most other educational institutions, is highly imperfect, and needs considerable change if it is to play an effective part in the education of children from the entire social range of the community. Where it is rigid and backward-looking, where it is unable to escape from a middle-class pre-occupation with conventional appearance and good manners, where its notions of culture are narrow and limited, it is disqualifying itself from meeting the needs of the intelligent children of the newer classes, who are clamouring to pass through its doors. This book is an attempt to discuss what must be the nature of the grammar school (or, indeed, of its successors where its work is taken over by other institutions), its curriculum, organisation and attitudes if it is to perform the function which society expects of it, in a time of rapid social change. This involves, inevitably, at least an implicit answer to the question what should we expect a liberal education to be in the 'sixties and 'seventies of this century.

The position of the grammar school in modern society is a crucial one. It stands at the meeting point of the élite and the popular cultures. Young men and women who wish for higher education will normally pass through its sixth form. Increasing numbers of children, whose families have had no experience of the grammar school and little of the cultural standards which they will be expected to assimilate there, are crowding into its courses. Many of these come from that large area of society which is occupied by what used to be thought of as lower middle and upper working classes, though it is doubtful if such terms are helpful under modern conditions, and it is certain that accurate description of class characteristics becomes increasingly impossible. It is to children from homes like these that the school must transmit our cultural heritage, and this book is largely concerned with the problems which are involved in this difficult task.

In their book, *Education and the Working Class*, Jackson and Marsden maintained that, in the grammar school, there is a necessary conflict between the standards of the middle and working classes. This seems to me an over-dramatisation of a complex and subtle social situation. In any case, many of these schools have already succeeded, demonstrably, in doing what these authors declare to be impossible. In fact they have an even more difficult duty to society, which remains, very largely, still to be faced. As the educational expectations of parents among the semi-skilled and unskilled manual workers catch up with those of their more affluent companions, a process which appears likely to take at least another generation, more and more children from an unprivileged background will come to the grammar school.

One last point remains to be mentioned. My emphasis so far, in discussing what society expects of the grammar school, has been on the work of diffusing throughout society the culture which we have received from the past. My own view is that this is a limited view of its opportunities. Modern scientific and technological developments have taken us into a period of rapid cultural change: the school then must educate children to live in an age of cultural innovation and, further, must prepare them to take part in the process by which this innovation comes about. It is no longer enough merely to accept a received culture. This involves us, at once, in a discussion of what is meant by the concept of culture itself, and of the implications for the grammar school of these new and formidable obligations—which some schools show no great desire to undertake.

Throughout this book I have made frequent reference to the school of which I was head master when it was being written—High Pavement School, Nottingham. I must make it clear that what I say should not be taken to refer to that school as it is in 1965.

3

# I

# *What do We Mean by Culture?*

TWO EMINENT American sociologists have stated that, in their review of definitions of culture in 1950, they had already found 164 definitions. By this time, no doubt, this number must have grown to more than 200. I do not intend to add one more to the number, but since there can hardly be a word in the English language which is used in so many different senses, it is important, especially in a book of this character, that when we use it we should be quite clear what we mean by it. What we have to watch for in particular, in many contemporary discussions, is a subtle and unannounced change in definition.

Writing in 1869, Matthew Arnold stated clearly his view of culture in his famous work *Culture and Anarchy*—'culture being a pursuit of our total perfection by means of getting to know, on all matters which most concern us, the best which has been thought and said in the world'. This perfectionist view has influenced many writers and thinkers, and is still important today. Two years later, the anthropologist Edward B. Tylor gave his definition—'culture or civilisation, taken in its widest ethnographic sense, is that complex whole which includes knowledge, belief, art, morals, law, custom and any other capabilities and habits acquired by man as a member of society'. The anthropological view of culture has developed in importance in this century, and it is now clear that the conception of culture as a way of life has triumphed over Arnold's 'sweetness and light'. T. S. Eliot, for example, who refuses to give a definition of culture, but prefers to offer notes towards its definition, means by it what the anthropologists mean; that is, a way of life of a particular people living together in one place. He adds significantly, however, that though this culture is made visible in their social system, their habits and customs, their art and their religion, it would be a mistake to think that it consists of these. Similarly, Raymond Williams accepts the view of culture as 'a whole way of life, material, intellectual and spiritual'.

At first sight, such a conception may seem far too vague and general to be useful, when we are considering culture in relation to an institution like the grammar school. In fact, there may be some who will be surprised to learn that it is possible for someone who is closely concerned with the grammar school to think of culture as anything other than the traditional notion of the cultivation of perfection, and of the graces of learning and gentility. There are indeed, in the grammar school, many who think that to be educated and to be cultured are identical terms, and in a sense this is, of course, true: it would be wrong, however, to say that it is impossible to be cultured unless one is educated in the accepted sense of that word.

Surely, in any complex society, it is inevitable that different cultural levels should emerge, if only because there are differences in intelligence, in insight and in responsiveness between its individual members. In this country, so far, the class system has limited the opportunity of many to aspire to the higher cultural levels, and it does not become the more fortunate minority to scorn those who have had fewer chances in life. Eliot thinks that, in an ideal culture, there should be a gradation of cultural levels, in which each person participates at the level appropriate to himself. Those at the top, so to speak, will have a more conscious culture and a greater specialisation of culture than those below, who will be more unconscious of their culture. The miner will differ from the artist, but in a healthy society they will both have a culture in common which they do not share with people of the same occupation in a foreign country. This common culture is based upon their language and literature, which implies thinking and feeling in common, and on their attitudes and pre-dispositions, many of which are below the level of consciousness.

What is clear, however, is that most of the major cultural advances in history have come from small groups of creative, dedicated persons. F. R. Cowell has pointed out that it needs

6

considerable capacity and energy even to formulate and understand the cultural tradition: it requires very much more to reshape and to add to it. Great intelligence and insight are as rare at one extreme, as great stupidity and mental deficiency at the other. Most of us are somewhere in the area between these two extremes, able to follow but hardly able to lead, though we must remind ourselves again and again that in our society there has always remained a great deal of undeveloped potentiality. The mass of men tend, then, to follow cultural standards set up by a creative minority, but a long way behind and a long time after. However much our fellow countrymen may disagree about political and religious matters, about Association and Rugby football, about the merits and demerits of television programmes broadcast by the BBC or ITV, yet the majority of Englishmen share a common respect for law and order, and a belief in democratic values. They insist on the right of the individual to express himself freely so long as, in doing so, he does not interfere with the rights of others. They expect a tolerant attitude towards the peculiarities of other Englishmen. All these, I take it, are aspects of their common way of life which we call their culture, even though much of this is more assumed and taken for granted than discussed and thought about. In so far as there is a cultural élite in our society, it exists in this context: it has no right to look down upon the rest of mankind as lesser breeds without the law, and still less must it attempt to impose its standards upon others. The leading scientist, the outstanding sculptor, the philosopher and the religious leader will each go ahead with his own work, doing his best to communicate with other men and women, but leaving them to accept or reject what he produces. In a civilised society, cultural standards must be dynamic not static. It is particularly important that there should be no cultural authority with the power to establish and fix standards, and so prevent development and progress. The innovator and the traditionalist are equally valuable in a community which is prepared to test all things and to hold fast only to what is good.

I do not find it difficult, then, to accept the view of culture as a whole way of life, granted that in a given society we may expect there to be many different cultural varieties and levels. I cannot sympathise with those who work for the establishment of a

7

common culture throughout society, in which everyone has the same standards and purposes. This conception seems to me one which constricts rather than one which liberates, and I can see no reason why there should not emerge a plurality of cultures, existing side by side in the same community. One argument against this is based on the danger, apparent enough in this country today, that such cultural differences may be entangled with social distinctions. I can see no reason, however, why the existence of different cultures should inevitably provide an occasion for social discrimination, even in this class-ridden country.

Since Richard Hoggart published *The Uses of Literacy* in 1957, it has become fashionable to base discussions of culture on the class hierarchy which emerged from the industrialisation of Britain during the nineteenth century, and to think in terms of a working-class culture and of middle-class values. This post-Marxist diagnosis has been pushed much farther by the disciples of Hoggart. In his fascinating and valuable book, Hoggart set himself the task of describing working-class culture as it was in a northern industrial area, when he was growing up in the nineteen-twenties and thirties, and the changes which have come about since then. His conclusion is that the influence of the 'mass publicists' has been in the direction of destroying much of 'the urban culture of the people' which still existed in the 'thirties, and that we are moving towards a mass culture. Hoggart says 'the old forms of class culture are in danger of being replaced by a poorer kind of classless, or by what I was led earlier to describe as a "faceless" culture, and this is to be regretted'. It might be added, too, that Hoggart was concentrating particularly on the printed word and that television is not even mentioned in his index. The powerful and almost universal influence of this medium of communication must surely reinforce his conclusion and lead us to believe that working-class culture is rapidly disappearing and is becoming a thing of the past.

It is appropriate to add that Hoggart's picture of working-class culture is deliberately limited by his own partial exclusion of what he calls 'the purposive, the political, the pious and the self-improving minorities of the working class'. A different picture might be painted of working-class culture in some parts of Leeds, even when Hoggart was growing up: this would emphasise the importance of the chapel as the centre of the activities of a group of families, and there is a distinct suggestion that the chapel played its part in producing social mobility: certainly many of the families which were prominent in its life seem to have 'got on'. Here again, after thirty years, there appears to have been a considerable decline in the importance of the chapel: its 'culture' is becoming submerged beneath the mass culture which surrounds it. It would be quite easy, too, to show the importance of the trade-union and of the 'Co-op' as a centre of working-class culture in northern and midland industrial areas at this time, to point out how they, too, were connected with the process by which families moved up in the social scale, and to find a similar falling-off in prominence today. Could it be that one important difference between 1930 and 1960 is that education has replaced other agencies as the chief factor in bringing about social mobility?

For my own part, then, I do not find it easy to regard working-class culture as playing any significant part in the life of the community today, though there are local exceptions and some vestigial remains. The brass band, pigeon fancying, the potent attractions of fish and chips are still with us; clogs, shawl, knur and spell have almost gone. In general, Light Programme, ITV, cinema, the popular Press, mass-produced advertisements and magazines are victorious, and local influences are giving way everywhere to national tendencies. The same forces are affecting the middle classes in precisely the same way, and are blurring the distinctions between working-class and middle-class attitudes and values. There are many people, indeed, who find it impossible to distinguish between working-class and lower middle-class.

Are these conceptions, too, rapidly becoming out of date? One result of technological change has been to produce an increase in non-manual employment: there are many more office and clerical workers. As industrial organisation becomes increasingly complex, there is a great need for men and women with technical and administrative skills. Society needs to employ far more people in insurance, banking, local government, the civil service. There has been a vast expansion in the distributive trades. The Registrar-General's divisions of society into five categories, professional and administrative class, clerical, skilled, semi-skilled and unskilled manual workers no longer appears particularly helpful. In the economic, as in the cultural field, the boundary line between working and middle class becomes increasingly difficult to find. Is there not a tendency to feel that we are all middle-class these days? At this moment in time, therefore, it is misleading and unhelpful to talk of a middle-class culture and of working-class values, without some attempt at close definition, and without remembering that the conceptions themselves are becoming out of date and are vanishing before our eyes.

The best attempt I know at such a definition appears in *The Uses of Literacy*. Hoggart points out here the importance of social solidarity, of 'togetherness' in working-class life, and of the influence of home, family and neighbourhood. He emphasises the self-respect, the stoicism and the tolerance of the working man. He shows a distrust of political life and politicians, and of established Christianity, a strong belief in fate and luck, a determination to concentrate on immediate pleasure and susceptibility to conformist group pressures. I have already indicated my view that this picture of working-class culture as it was earlier in the century is an incomplete one, and that it is, in any case, out of date today. What remains to be pointed out is a tendency towards a romanticisation of the old working-class values and of the so-called 'organic society' which existed before industrialisation set in. The myth of the noble working-man has replaced the earlier one of the noble savage. There must always have been something limiting and frustrating about working-class culture, even as described by Hoggart, and it is fascinating to find the heroine of Wesker's play *Roots* achieving maturity by escaping from the cramping influences of her working-class background— 'it does work, it's happening to me, I can feel it's happened, I'm beginning, on my own two feet—I'm beginning'.

It is notable that those who tend to romanticise the working classes make little attempt to define with precision what they imagine middle-class values to be. An attack on social snobbery, comments on acquisitiveness and excessive individualism, sneers at pretentiousness and pomposity hardly do justice to such a vast subject. Indeed, I doubt the usefulness of even attempting a definition, because it seems to me that the expression middle-class covers such a vast area of British society that generalisation becomes impossible.

Our society is, indeed, in a state of flux, and the traditional class differences seem to be disappearing quickly. It is possible,

## What do We Mean by Culture?

I think, to detect the gradual emergence of three cultural groups, which for convenience I shall call the Establishment (not that this is particularly new), the Intelligentsia and the Majority (I do not admire this expression, but use it because of its comparative neutrality). The Establishment needs only a brief description: prosperous, orthodox, Church of England, public school and conventional Oxbridge, middlebrow. Its members might be expected to read *The Times*, the *Sunday Times*, *The Spectator*, the *Daily* and *Sunday Telegraph*, to appreciate the West End theatre, to be baffled by the modern movement in the arts and architecture, to be both Conservative and conservative. They hold a great number of important positions in the community and have a long tradition of service. Their ranks are continually augmented by those who have achieved success through their education or their financial, commercial and industrial activities. This is the group which regards itself as divinely appointed to rule, and regards any interference with this right as an interruption in the workings of the law of Nature.

The Intelligentsia has emerged since the First World War largely through grammar school and university (very much including Oxbridge), though many ex-public school boys and self-educated people are to be found in its ranks. Its members have escaped, equally, from the stuffy conventionality of the middle-class and the stifling and limited working-class background. They might be expected to be interested in the arts in general and the modern movement in particular, and to read *The Guardian*, *The Observer*, the *New Statesman* (though they will find, in at least one of these, occasional infuriating remnants of travel, fashion and educational snobbery—witness the fashion correspondent who, in May 1962, implored her readers to buy their shoes in either Rome or New York). A strong element in this group is scientifically educated: many will be humanist rather than religious, and it is likely that there will be a considerable questioning of orthodoxy in the sphere of morals, politics and the arts. An experimental attitude towards life in general and an agnosticism about received values are typical. If there is to be found in this country a cultural élite, in the sense to which T. S. Eliot refers, this is presumably it, though many of its characteristics can hardly meet with Eliot's approval. To a large extent, the Intelligentsia exists outside social class: it points

11

towards the classless society imagined and hoped for by liberal idealists for many generations.

Popular, Majority culture, with its influence which pervades all levels of society, presumably needs little detailed description. It is a commonplace to read anguished attacks on the influences of television, cinema, radio, the popular Press, cheap magazines, advertisements, football pools, hire purchase and the low standards of the popular entertainment industry. It has become fashionable to deplore the commercialism of the 'candy-floss world', the worship of the new-fangled, the cynicism, the escape from life, the soggy romanticism, the concentration on sex and on violence which are so obviously found in the majority culture. Hoggart himself summarises it all when he says 'we are encouraging a sense, not of the dignity of each person but of a new aristocracy, the monstrous regiment of the flat-faced'. Raymond Williams, looking at the matter from the angle of those who control these communications points out that 'control of the new forces passes to men who are not interested in the growth of society, or in the human purposes the expansion is serving. . . . Instead of a new culture emerging, a synthetic culture will be devised for a quick sale'.

Modern inventions like television and cinema have not created low standards: they have merely revealed how low existing standards were. The new techniques contain within themselves the promise of improvement in the future: they are themselves neutral. Everything depends upon who controls them, and the use which is made of them. There are encouraging as well as discouraging tendencies. If it is important to spread far and wide the knowledge of some new agricultural technique, the most effective method is to show its use by a favourite character in *The Archers*. Popular television programmes can do a great deal to undermine a fear of hospitals, and to spread understanding of the nature of mental illness and of psychological treatment. Is it beyond the realm of possibility that a successor of *Z Cars* might make a positive contribution to more satisfactory attitudes towards crime? Mass society is not seeking culture but entertainment, but the boundaries between these are not always sharply defined.

There has been a great increase in the reading of 'better' newspapers, periodicals and books: the tremendous prolifera-

## What do We Mean by Culture?

tion of paperbacks has brought within the reach of thousands works of great literature and books of quality in all departments of human knowledge. A similar development has taken place in the use of public libraries, colleges of Further Education and that valuable institution the Village College. Even small towns can boast of their musical and dramatic societies: any large town will show a remarkable blossoming of cultural groups, hobbies and leisure-time activities. A significant proportion of films, and of radio and television programmes, are valuable, which is as much as could have been claimed for the novels written in the nineteenth century. Good repertory theatres are more than holding their own (some of them are even achieving a new home): audiences for concerts of classical music, ballet, opera and good jazz are bigger than they have ever been. An increasing number of working-class families now own cars and take continental holidays: more and more of their children are staying at school to 16, or are obtaining admission to the grammar school and going on to higher education. A typical case is that of a working man, with a son at the local grammar school, who heard a broadcast discussion about careers and higher education: he suddenly came to the conclusion that his son would be robbed of his rights if he did not go to University.

Any division of society into cultural groups, like that attempted earlier, is in a sense arbitrary, and there is a great deal of overlapping, with nothing clear-cut and defined. The same person will be found with a foot in at least two of the camps: many of us who like to think of ourselves as members of the Intelligentsia are greatly influenced by the popular culture, and the contrary is equally true. It is appropriate to indicate the particular importance of the grammar school at this point, since it is very much concerned both with the emergence of the Intelligentsia and with the border-line between that group and the Majority. Its task is a very difficult one on that particular border-line, and also because it is much involved with the new teenage sub-culture which has grown up so rapidly in the last decade and has had widespread effects across the boundaries of the traditional social classes.

In one sense, the attitudes and leisure-time activities of the teenager represent merely a special case of the popular majority culture. Young people can hardly help being influenced strongly

13

by the mass media of communication, and provide a profitable market for those who wish to sell pop records, magazines and films. With their great spending power, they offer an easy target for the ingenious advertiser who will allow no scruple to stand in the way of a quick profit. Their determination to show themselves grown up leads them to imitate the most striking features of the adult life which they see around them, and one must say that they find little which places a great strain on their intelligence. An interesting feature of the situation, however, is the gradual development of a self-conscious teenage outlook. We are well accustomed to the adolescent who, at one and the same time, finds it possible to rebel against adult standards and to make himself as much like a grown-up as he possibly can. What is new is the common feeling that young people are, so to speak, a race apart, with their own characteristics, opinions, standards and even uniform. Communication between teenager and adult seems to be increasing in difficulty, and the grown-up who wishes to cross the gulf has to think very carefully about the nature of his approaches—not that this, in itself, is at all a bad thing. Whatever may be the cause of the development, and it is probably connected with the attempt of part of the adult world to regard young people as a special market either for its goods or for its so-called cultural products, it certainly introduces a complicating factor into a discussion of what we mean by culture. At a critical stage in their growth, young people from all kinds of social and economic backgrounds are being subjected to many common influences (has not a writer in *The Observer* stated that the clothing to be worn by the upper-class 'miss' is determined by the ex-secondary modern school girl when she begins to earn at 15?). Although some of these influences are those which I have called the Majority culture, some are interesting developments from it. Self-conscious group questioning of adult standards, as contrasted with the individual questioning so common among adolescents, may produce some results which will be fascinating especially to those of us who feel that there is much in modern Britain which needs a vigorous examination. The addiction to pop music may settle into a permanent habit, or it could grow into an interest in jazz and other musical forms, including classical music. The adventurous and active spirit of the young, expressed in their holidays, their sporting and leisure-

14

time activities (for those most seriously afflicted by the television drug are rarely to be found in this age-group) may well produce results which are invaluable both to the individuals concerned and to the community as a whole. It is encouraging when a group of young people quite voluntarily band themselves together to serve old-age pensioners by visiting them and doing jobs for them, with the stated object of doing something to mitigate their loneliness The world of the mature—or is that too strong a claim?—need not be altogether depressed by the activities of the younger generation who, as ever, will respond to the right kind of encouragement and help, though this implies encouragement and help on their own terms. The strong support among young people for the Campaign for Nuclear Disarmament—and whether one supports the campaign or not, it is surely encouraging to find youth actively on the side of peace and life, rather than of war and death—may be set against the lack of interest in politics of others.

A discussion of our culture at this moment in time would, I suppose, be incomplete without some reference to Sir Charles Snow's Rede Lecture *The Two Cultures and the Scientific Revolution*. In so far as 'The Two Cultures' is a statement of an educational problem, few would disagree with it: there is an obvious need for the literary intellectual (and the man in the street) to be aware of the methods and achievements of modern science and also for the scientists to know more about literature, the arts and the humanities. In another part of this book I attempt to discuss some of the things which can be done, and are already being done in many schools, in this connection.

When, however, we examine Snow's view of culture, we move on to more difficult ground. Snow says 'at one pole, the scientific culture really is a culture, not only in an intellectual but also in an anthropological sense', and again 'there are common attitudes, common standards and patterns of behaviour, common approaches and assumptions. This goes surprisingly wide and deep. It cuts across other mental patterns, such as those of religion or politics or class.' I, for one, should deny the validity of such a claim for a scientific culture, and even if it were true it surely gives only a limited view of what a culture implies. It is not necessary to go the whole way with Leavis to feel that a culture which excludes the arts is no culture at all, either in an intellectual or an anthropological sense. In any case, in a highly developed and complex civilisation, do we not look for as many different attitudes and approaches as possible within the framework of the values which all accept? May not the intuition, awareness and insights of the artist and writer tell us more than the scientist can even about the effects of scientific inventions on the lives of men and women?

Is not Snow really drawing attention to the fact that our culture has now become so wide and complex that it has become almost impossible for one man to be familiar with more than a few of its different aspects? At a high level, specialisation is unavoidable, and it is by no means only in the sciences that one specialist finds it difficult to understand the activities of another. What surely needs our attention more than all this is the stock of common values which forms the bases of our culture, and here we have to rely on the philosophers, the men of religion and the artists. As has been well said in *The Spectator* 'Knowledge is power, but it is not the knowledge of how that power should be used.' A. N. Whitehead develops this point further when he says 'Now wisdom is the way in which knowledge is held. It concerns the handling of knowledge, its selection for the determination of relevant issues, its employment to add value to our immediate experience.'

To summarise, my view of culture as a whole way of life must include all the arts, all the sciences, historical and geographical influences, philosophy, psychology, religion, political and social theory; in fact, the whole body of learning with, in addition, the experience of the human race which is embodied in its institutions, manners, social customs, leisure activities and the like, and much of this will be beneath the level of consciousness. There are, and will remain, different kinds of culture, and we should avoid the temptation to arrange these in a hierarchy, with our own special category at the top, though we have to recognise that some have more value than others. The danger is that these kinds of culture may become attached to different social classes, as they have done in this country in the past, though there is no necessity why this should be so. Indeed, there are many signs that class distinctions are rapidly losing their importance and are being replaced by more flexible cultural groupings, and we have found traces of three such groupings which we have called the Establishment, the Intelligentsia and the Majority Culture.

It is not yet possible to assume that the majority culture must necessarily be low in taste: there is no need to adopt threatening attitudes to defend the ark of the covenant against the assaults of the mob. Technical changes have got well ahead of educational developments. We have to agree that the present situation offers a strong temptation to those who control mass communications to make a profit out of the ignorance and inexperience of the majority, and to exploit what we hope is only a transitional culture by appeals to the baser elements in human nature. I have given reasons why it is not necessary to despair of the popular culture, and it may be that, when the grandchildren of the teenagers of today are themselves at school, a very different picture may appear of the cultural standards in our society. Much depends, indeed, on the standards of those who are responsible for the popular Press, commercial television and the film industry.

Cultural equality is impossible: it is inconceivable that everyone should read *The Guardian*, enjoy Beethoven or visit the theatre to see Shakespeare's plays. There is a strong tendency among educated people to assume that only the highly literate can be cultured and to forget that there are many other forms of creative activity. Raymond Williams reminds us of the value of 'not only the cognate forms of theatre, concert and picture gallery, but a whole range of general skills from gardening, metalwork and carpentry to active politics'. What we should be working towards is a state of society in which the attitudes of the most cultivated would be, if not accepted fully by everybody, at least tolerated willingly and not jeered at or ignored. Professor Jeffreys has pointed out the need for a cultural tradition which would have the same authority in the sphere of social values and the arts as it has with regard to science and technology. The cultural élite, which would both maintain this tradition from generation to generation and at the same time initiate new tendencies and fresh developments, must be very fluid socially and would in fact be the 'Intelligentsia' which we have already discussed. Side by side with this, we need a rapid growth, already in evidence in many localities, of more and more voluntary cultural associations, in which men and women of all levels of education can develop their personal interests and learn to take responsibility. Is it only my own prejudice and interest as an educationalist which make me see these matters as largely educational problems? Although it is clear to me that the grammar school has to play an important part in their solution, yet I must emphasise at this point that I mean education in its fullest sense and not mere schooling—that process of growth and maturing which begins at school but should continue throughout life.

## 2

# *The 'First-Generation' Grammar School Boy*

SINCE THE Second World War, particularly in urban areas, teachers in grammar schools have become increasingly conscious of the influx into their schools of children who are the first members of their family to obtain entrance. When neither of his parents, nor any of his brothers or sisters, have attended grammar school, it is likely that a child may find the expectations and attitudes of the school difficult to understand. It would, of course, be absurd to suggest that this is a new problem. The rapid development of secondary education, and its spread into new areas of society, must obviously have been bringing first-generation grammar school children into the maintained schools ever since the 1902 Education Act was put into operation. At the end of the First World War, I entered a small co-educational 'secondary school' in the West Riding of Yorkshire which was just beginning to develop quickly, and like many of my contemporaries I was the first member of my family to undergo such an experience, having won a place as a scholarship boy. Since the 1944 Education Act, the abolition of fee-paying and the establishment of free secondary education for all have brought a great influx of such children into the grammar school, though it should be said that in many industrial cities, including Nottingham, free secondary education was well on the way before 1939. In less progressive parts of the country, the first-generation child had found himself in a minority, and had to be absorbed slowly into the majority group of children whose families were well accustomed to this type of schooling and probably had much more money than his. Today there are many schools, including High Pavement School, in which at least half of the new pupils may be expected to be the first members of their families to come to a grammar school.

Maintained grammar schools in industrial areas, and those which serve the 'poorer' areas of large cities, will normally expect this kind of proportion among their new pupils. Where a school caters for a residential area, or through the operation of a particular kind of selective system of preferences is able to choose its own entrants, it is more likely that only a minority of its entry will be first-generation pupils. It would be surprising if direct-grant schools, or independent day schools with their built-in opportunities to 'cream' the maintained school, did not find themselves in the same position. No one can generalise about 'the grammar school'—though many try to do so—and it is difficult to paint a convincing picture of its social constitution. Each school must be seen against its own background. If accurate thinking is to be at all possible, we must take into account the nature of the area which it serves (urban, rural, residential, industrial or some mixture of these) of local policy for the selection and distribution of children at 11 (is there a system of geographical zoning or are parents allowed to choose the school they would prefer?), of the varying prestige of the schools in question. Even in the same city, it is possible for two schools to be dealing with a substantially different sort of problem. Can one speak in the same breath of the educational tasks of Manchester Grammar School and Smoketown Grammar School?

In their book *Education and the Working Class*, Jackson and Marsden have examined many of the effects of the entry of the first-generation grammar school child, though they have preferred to deal with the matter in terms of class. I have already pointed out that I did not find it easy to divide my pupils, or their parents, into working class and middle class. No matter whether I pay attention to accent, dress, cultural interests, leisure-time occupations or apparent income group, such a class division seems to me to have become largely artificial and out of date. I recognise that some families have more money than others, live in a 'poorer' area, or earn their money by manual work, though usually I have to be told these things: what I do not recognise is that these families have a class attitude to the school which makes them different from the people whose homes, occupations and incomes may generally be thought to be superior. Nor do I find that their children have a noticeably greater or smaller difficulty in fitting into school. In my experience, the most easily recognisable and most significant difference is between those families which are well-accustomed to the school and its ways and those who are not, and between those boys whose parents or brothers and sisters have attended grammar school and those whose relatives have not. In other words, I find the conception of first-generation grammar school boy helpful and meaningful, and that of working-class boy confusing and nebulous. I may add that, early in my teaching career, I found it easy to think in the same terms as Jackson and Marsden.

Before I discuss the particular problems which arise from the presence of so many first-generation children in the grammar school, I shall consider *Education and the Working Class* in some detail, partly because so many people appear to regard it as an authoritative statement about 'the grammar school', and partly because it touches upon so many of the topics with which I shall be dealing.

*Education and the Working Class* consists largely of a survey of the experiences and attitudes of ten middle-class children and eighty-eight working-class children, who passed in the Higher School Certificate or at Advanced Level in four grammar schools in a northern industrial city between 1949 and 1952 (extended to 1954 for a few of the girls who are included). Evidence was obtained from school records, conversations with parents and with the pupils when they had grown up, and it is quite clear to anyone with experience of young people of this sort that much of this evidence is convincing and has the ring of truth. Doubt enters, however, when we come to examine the generalisations which are drawn from the evidence, and the assumptions which are made with very few facts behind them. The authors state that they themselves might properly be considered among the eighty-eight cases, and soon there comes a point at which it is difficult to avoid a feeling that even the evidence may be affected by the questions asked and the attitudes and opinions of those who ask them. Just as in certain B.B.C. programmes, for which 'actuality-material' about opinions and attitudes is collected, the researchers do not find it hard to discover what they are looking for. However, it has to be said that pre-conceived ideas, so strongly held that they are outside the range of testing by mere facts, are no part of the equipment of a scientific sociologist.

The conclusions of the book may be summarised in the author's own words. The grammar school has 'foundered on a rock: the working class' (p. 215). 'The grammar school has now to address itself to a new public: but could it, even if it so wished?' (p. 215). 'Every custom, every turn of phrase, every movement of judgment, informs the working-class parent and the working-class child that the grammar schools do not "belong" to them' (p. 215). 'Grammar schools are so socially imprisoned that they are most remarkable for the conformity of the minds they train' (p. 219). The general verdict is that the grammar school is an incurably middle-class institution which is incapable of transmitting the central culture of our society to the working-class majority: it must be replaced by the comprehensive school.

In examining this thesis, it is necessary to re-emphasise that all grammar schools are not alike, either in their attitudes and policies or in their social constitution. It may well be that there are some grammar schools which are unwelcoming to working-class children, but, as I have pointed out, the proportion of first generation children differs very much from school to school. It seems inconceivable to me that a school which takes more than 50 per cent of such children each year should be so obtuse as not to notice the fact and allow its policy to be affected by it. Further, even if it were true that all four schools in Huddersfield had not learned to gear themselves to an increasing proportion of working-class children between 1948 and 1952, it does not follow that the same thing is true of them today, and even less that one can generalise about all or most grammar schools in the country on the slender basis of what one thought one saw in four of their number more than ten years ago.

In fact, much of what the book discusses is already out of date. The last decade has seen a tremendous increase in the number of working-class children (to argue in the same terms as the authors) who have stayed into the sixth form of the grammar school quite voluntarily, who are obviously very much more at home there, and are there because they like it. Long before 1949, however, there were many grammar schools in the country which were

dealing happily with this situation. I was myself educated, in the
nineteen-twenties, at a school quite near to Huddersfield, and
in common with many others had no great difficulty with
'alien' standards. In my experience, all schools had their peculiar
ways and one just had to get used to them. Later on, of course,
there emerged the occasional person with a chip on his shoulder,
who is to be found in all human institutions. The majority of
pupils, both in my own school and in that which I know best
now, were and are neither the 'odd men out' nor the abject conformists into which Jackson and Marsden divide the 'Marburton'
pupils. One can easily see, of course, how a boy like Leslie Barron
could have a disruptive influence on his associates (p. 104-5).

There are, indeed, differences in the atmosphere of many
homes and many schools. Any school which seeks to enlarge the
experience of its pupils, to encourage a sense of personal responsibility and to develop discrimination, will inevitably place some
pupils in a position in which they first sense and ultimately
become fully conscious of a contrast between the standards of
home and neighbourhood on the one hand and of school on the
other. It will happen in the comprehensive school as well as in
the grammar school. It has nothing particularly to do with
working-class homes and pupils: it may well be even more
serious in the case of a well-to-do self-made man, who feels inclined to reach for his gun when he hears the word culture.

The first tensions may be felt when the child needs to do homework, in a house which has only one heated room which is
devoted to the great god television. The development of an
interest in books, classical music, the theatre or politics, in an
atmosphere to which all this is completely alien, can lead to considerable conflict: I well remember a sixth-former whose parents
would not allow him to listen to the Third Programme. Any
school will wish to teach its pupils to speak correctly (and here I
am concerned not with accent but with a response to such a
question as 'Shall we need us football boots?'). The effect of a
mode of speech, which has departed from the ungrammatical
and lazy norm, can easily be imagined on friends and not very
sympathetic brothers and sisters, and it is not surprising that
many intelligent grammar school pupils become bi-lingual. The
point, however, is not that such tensions and difficulties exist,
but that they may arise whenever and wherever children are

developing new sides to their personality and are enlarging their interests.

A much more deeply rooted problem is presented by the linguistically deprived children who come from many homes. A number of researchers, including notably Basil Bernstein, have pointed out the many children, particularly from the families of unskilled working men, whose performance in verbal reasoning tests fails to represent their real ability. Some children develop only slowly in reading and writing, their thinking is mainly descriptive, and they find it difficult to form abstract conceptions. Inside their own homes, they rarely hear or take part in discussion, and their social relationships do little to stimulate either their vocabulary or their ability to express their thoughts. It is for this reason among others that numbers of children from 'poorer' homes fail to achieve entry into the grammar school or into the selective forms of other schools. Unless the primary school is able, and it is a difficult task, to provide the missing stimulus, children who are potentially well able to cope with grammar school work will be deprived of the opportunity even to try.

Among those children who secure admission to the grammar school, however, we find a number who are still verbally restricted, and this presents a particular difficulty as school work becomes more academic, abstract and formal. These are the pupils who fail English Language and French at O Level, while showing considerable ability in Mathematics and the Sciences. Their written English shows a limited vocabulary; they tend to write short, simple sentences joined together by conjunctions and make little use of subordinate clauses. They are at their inadequate best when describing concrete situations or events which they have experienced themselves, but they are often at a loss when required to write an imaginative essay or to make a coherent consecutive statement. Many of these pupils, if left to their own devices, will read little, since reading is both an unusual and an unpopular occupation at home. If they do read, they will often confine themselves to descriptive books about science. The grammar school, then, has much to do if these children are to be helped to escape from the limitations of their background into complete articulateness. Among the characteristics which we should expect to find in the fully mature and well-educated person must surely be included a capacity for deep

24

thought, unhampered by an inability to think in abstract terms, and the ability to express these thoughts in both speech and writing. In other words, education in any effective sense implies articulacy. It is easy to see the tensions which might arise in the life of a particular child while he is learning these new techniques of thought and expression against an uncomprehending and unsympathetic background.

One other consideration may well arise. When the school is attempting to encourage its pupils to be articulate, to join in discussions and to express points of view which are strongly held, it is likely that some of its pupils will appear argumentative, brash and even crude. The abject conformity referred to by Jackson and Marsden, as characteristic of the working-class boy who is making a success of his career in the grammar school, was not one of the most outstanding attributes of the boys of High Pavement School. Members of staff are sometimes appalled by the frank, outspoken comments of their pupils, and may even relapse into the usual condemnation of an entire generation of young people. A greater faith in their own ability to distinguish between impudence and a genuine lack of familiarity with accepted forms of speech, together with a greater understanding of the needs of the developing adolescent, would surely serve to diminish friction and solace outraged feelings.

In many cases the problem is exacerbated by the complication of conflicts inside the home background itself. Under these circumstances, schoolmasters and mistresses may suffer because of the hostility of the pupil to all adult authority. Here, however, is no occasion for shocked horror: the delicate task of helping an angry adolescent to merge comparatively whole from his unsettled period is one which needs tact, understanding and a deep human sympathy. The work of healing is not assisted by the brash pomposity of an enraged colleague who is himself suffering from an overdose of immaturity. It should be remembered, too, that those who find it difficult to become amenable are those pupils with considerable strength of character, those in fact who have a great contribution to make both to the life of the school and of society at large. Strong-minded adolescents will not be reconciled by repressive methods or by stuffy conventional regulations, and an undue interest in the length of their hair, the narrowness of their trousers and the pointedness of their shoes is almost calculated to bring out the worst in their natures. It must not be thought, however, that such young people are to be regarded as beyond criticism. Everything depends upon how the criticism is given and who it is given by. There are some teachers who should almost be disqualified from attempting such criticisms: on the other hand, even the most aggressive sea-lawyer among the apparently subversive element in a school will receive the most astringent criticism if it is given by someone he respects and likes. The immature sixth-former, trying to find himself in his confused personal and social situation, should surely be able to rely on the interest, the understanding and, if necessary, the benevolent disapproval of those whose job it is to help him to educate himself. It is remarkable how soon some adults can contrive to forget their own feelings and difficulties at the age of 16. What is required of them is no attitude of soft, sloppy sentimentality but an insistance upon high standards of work and behaviour, combined with those good personal relations which will enable the teenager both to respect and to like them.

Many children will grow away from their parents to some extent, will find that they have little to talk to them about and appear to have little in common.[1] In some cases parents are sensitive enough to be able to develop some way with their children and to join in some of their new interests—and I have known some who have become supporters of Nottingham Playhouse because their sons have become interested in drama. Even where this is not possible, the gradual divergence of parent and son can come about happily, with the parent fully conscious of what is taking place, and with no loss of mutual affection. Discord between parent and developing adolescent is obviously not confined to the so-called working-classes—almost every parent is conscious of the conflict of the generations at some point or another—though contrasts of age and education can interact and exacerbate each other. What can be expected, of course, is that the school itself should be conscious of these difficulties and should be using all its skill and experience to mitigate their effects. Schools which are doing nothing to help, or which are sublimely unconscious of the existence of a problem, are thoroughly bad schools. Where one disagrees with Jackson and Marsden is in

[1] See Appendix 1 for a short play, written by a schoolboy, which expresses this point very clearly.

their view that the grammar school is not attempting to help, and is, by its very nature, disqualified from achieving success.

At this moment in its history, the grammar school is particularly involved in the process by which individuals move up the social ladder. The intelligent boy who is successful at school and moves on to University may acquire an income, a standard of living and a place in society which are far beyond anything of which his father ever dreamed: it is even possible that he might become manager of the very coal mine at which his father is a miner. It does not follow, however, because success in a grammar school leads straight to what society regards as a middle-class occupation that the grammar school must be a middle-class institution: success in a comprehensive school has precisely the same result, and I have yet to learn that comprehensive schools are ineradicably middle-class. The grammar school is not responsible for the English class system: it exists in a society which has been dominated by class consciousness, though happily social distinctions are gradually coming to mean less and less, and through no fault of its own it has become the main agent in bringing about social mobility. This is a fact to which its pupils have to learn to adjust themselves: after all, part of the process of maturing is to learn to adapt oneself to different kinds of environment. It is a tribute to all concerned that, in many schools, this adjustment is accomplished happily and with the minimum of friction and bitterness.

What then can the grammar school do to welcome and encourage those who come to it either from working-class homes, or without any previous knowledge of what it expects and what it is trying to do? Jackson and Marsden refer (p. 104) to 'the common images of "dominance" or "leadership": school uniform, teachers' gowns, prefects, the Honours Board, the First XI, the Scout Troop, the School Corps, Speech Day, Morning Assembly, Expected Public Decorum'. It is possible to agree with them that excessive emphasis on all this can be positively unwelcoming to those who have never met it before. Need it be pointed out, however, that many schools are able to keep a sense of proportion, and that the symbols mentioned find a place in many different types of schools? (except the School Corps which exists only in a small minority of grammar schools and in independent schools). All schools are required by law to have a School

Assembly and no doubt attempt to make the fullest educational use of it. Which schools fail to play matches against other schools? How many schools have no prefects, no prizes, no Speech Days, no school uniform and no concern for the behaviour of their pupils in public? It is remarkable if these symbols inevitably produce an atmosphere completely alien to the working class, since they are to be found rampant throughout the primary and secondary schools of the country.

The grammar school needs to be receptive, permissive and tolerant: it must aim, consciously and positively, at removing the difficulties in the way of the first-generation grammar school child.

There are indeed, far too many stuffy, conventional and hidebound grammar schools which are still aping the independent schools. These are the schools which are concerned to produce young ladies or gentlemen, which are obsessed with the appearance of gentility, and with the difference between 'U' and 'non U', and if all schools were like these one could see the force of the criticisms. There are, however, many ways in which one can test the attitude of the school towards children who come from less-cultivated homes. What, for example, is the policy of the school towards school uniform? A sense of proportion which limits the emphasis on uniform is surely indicated, and one does not need to be a dangerous revolutionary to regard a school cap as a ludicrous object on the head of a large boy or a gym tunic as unbecoming to the adolescent girl. A foolscap sheet of instructions about how to wear a school cap, and such a thing has been heard of, is a sign of a loss of a sense of proportion somewhere. Many children need to acquire standards of cleanliness and neatness and a pride in their personal appearance, and at a certain stage in their development school uniform often helps. Beyond this it has little importance, and uniformity for its own sake has little value. Is school uniform really necessary for the sixth-former?

A school may also be judged by its attitude towards games. If games are compulsory, is there a genuine range of options, available at least to the senior pupils? Since many boys, and even more girls, think that chasing a ball is a pointless and ridiculous activity, is some other form of physical activity available? There is a danger that children will indulge in an excessive worship of

28

successful games players: is it not a sign of delayed adolescence when members of staff do the same? Other interesting questions are, what proportion of the prefects are poor games players, and with which schools are fixtures arranged, It is possible to judge of the social pretensions of a school by an examination of its fixture list. To sum up, games must not be allowed to become a fetish: cricket, for example, can be either an enjoyable game or a religion. Why must games be compulsory for sixth-formers?

What is the school's policy towards youth clubs and part-time employment? Obviously a grammar school pupil may spend far too much time on his youth club (or any other activity), may neglect his homework and ruin his prospects at school. It has always seemed to me that the way to deal with this situation is not to frown on membership of all clubs, but to enlist the help of the club leader. A youth club offers still another valuable field for the exercise of leadership and the development of interests, and a school has no exclusive rights over the leisure of its pupils. A working alliance with the club leader may bring great benefits both to club and pupil. Similarly, it seems to me wrong to ban part-time employment. I have every respect for a boy who wishes to stand on his own feet and who is unhappy to see his parents sacrifice for his benefit while he makes no contribution. It has to be remembered too that the boy or girl who is in the sixth form suffers badly in comparison with one who leaves school at 15 or 16, in the way of pocket money and access to adolescent delights. I was much impressed by a boy who said to me, 'I won't stay into the sixth form, because it means that my mother will have to go on working: she's not fit to do it, and I won't let her.' To avoid such a situation, it seems to me that the boy should be allowed to work, even if he has a maintenance grant. It seems to me that that uses to which a boy puts his leisure time is very much a matter to be decided by his parents and himself. It is important, of course, that school permission shall be obtained, and that the amount of time spent should be regulated: a proper scheme, supported by the local authority, can be very rewarding and there is no reason why it should be confined to sixth-formers. I cannot see that a paper-round need do a boy any harm, so long as the parents understand that the school has the power to withdraw permission if his work deteriorates. Where a boy is needed for a school team, difficulties can arise. Some sort of compromise can usually be worked out if both parties are co-operative, and the boy is far more likely to be co-operative if the school is not trying to prevent him from having his job. After all, some boys are ingenious enough to avoid this situation by keeping out of school teams. Is it really a sign of disloyalty towards his school if a pupil prefers to play for the team of a Youth Club, in a game which he enjoys more than the one provided at school? or if he attends evening activities at his club in preference to school clubs and societies? or if he earns his own pocket-money by having a part-time job? A stern inflexible attitude in these matters can cause an amount of friction which may distract the head of a school quite seriously from his more important functions and duties.

As far as Expected Public Decorum is concerned, again a sense of proportion is required. To eat chips or ice-cream in the street, while wearing school uniform, seems to me neither the sin against the Holy Ghost which our traditionalists appear to think it, nor an indispensable symbol of a success revolt against grammar school standards. On the other hand, any school will be interested in the way its pupils behave when they are boarding buses or walking through the streets in a group. It is part of their social training to learn to behave with consideration for other people, and to be courteous and helpful. If no one else has taught them this, the school must, but no sensible person expects children in groups always to behave properly and the school must take some responsibility for what happens when its pupils are together in the outside world.

In all these ways, then, the grammar school can (and very often does) avoid giving an impression of orthodox stodginess and inflexibility. The school should go very much farther than this, however, in its attempt to provide a congenial atmosphere for pupils who are making a first contact with this sort of school. Different schools have worked out their own ways of doing this: what follows is a description of what is done in one school.

On the first day on which he attends school, the boy is handed over by his parents to his senior house master, and so from the start they know personally the master who is to be responsible for their son's welfare. They are encouraged to write to him and to make appointments to see him. If he feels it wise, he will invite parents to come and see him: in exceptional cases, he may even visit them in their own homes. Throughout the boy's career, his house master looks after him and in many cases gets to know him well. The boy always has someone to whom he can turn when in difficulty: he may appeal to his house master, for example, if he feels that he has been unjustly punished.

In the first year, there is no attempt to divide the boys into different ability groups, and boys go together from the same primary school into the same form without any grading. 'Streaming' come about gradually and is not completed until the fourth year (see Chapter 3). During the first year, the form master plays an important part in welcoming the new boy to the school, in teaching him its customs and ways, and in helping him through what is often a difficult transition period. He is given time in which to do this each week, and an attempt is made to find masters who are able to teach more than one subject to fill the position of first-form masters. A boy who, in his primary school, has been taught by one teacher for most of the time, is often bewildered to receive the attentions of seven or eight subject specialists. The 11-year-old has also to learn quickly that he will be taught different subjects in different places in the school, and has to accustom himself to turning up in the proper room, with the appropriate equipment, at the right time. Add to this the fact that he may well have been a person of some importance in his last school, whereas in his new one he is the lowest form of life, and it can easily be seen why some boys take a long time to settle in their new school. In addition, High Pavement School was organised in such a way that the deputy headmaster had a particular responsibilty for first and second-year boys: he interviewed parents instead of the headmaster, presided at first and second form parents' meetings, signed the boys' reports and in all ways acted as their headmaster.

One of the charges which Jackson and Marsden bring against the 'Marburton' grammar schools is their failure, indeed their inability, to give adequate information to parents about courses in the school, about subject options and their connections with future careers and about the complicated business of University entrance. It is imperative that parents should feel interested in the school and welcome when they visit it; in fact, that it is 'their' school and not one which their sons happen to attend through an accident of geography. If a parent arrives at school, she should be seen whether or not she has made an appointment (and it is generally a mother): if the matter she has in mind is important enough to bring her to school, it is important that she should be seen.

In this particular school, a strong Parent–Staff Association has been built up over the years: many parents are known personally to masters, and every attempt has been made to create an encouraging atmosphere in which parents feel at home in the school. (In parenthesis, it may be added that I share none of the fears, which many heads obviously feel, that such an Association may attempt to interfere in school policy. I had nothing but the friendliest co-operation from the Association, which helped the school by making innumerable gifts and by establishing the happiest relationship between home and school.)

As the boy moved up the school, a great effort was made to give the parents information about courses, options and their implications as far as careers were concerned. Letters were sent home, courses were discussed at meetings of parents of boys in the appropriate age-group and questions answered, though it was usually found that the simplest and quickest way to get the information across was to give it clearly to the boy, and to follow that by a written communication. If, unfortunately, a boy has embarked on the wrong course or if he changes his mind, and boys may develop quite unexpectedly, the school must take a great deal of trouble to improvise a special timetable for him: the smoothness of the organisation must give way to the needs of the boy. Questions of careers and the possibility of a boy staying into the sixth form were raised early in the fourth year, and the fourth-form Parents' Meeting was largely concerned with these questions. In the majority of cases, it is the boy who decides that he wishes to stay on at school and tells his parents this. I have had many visits from parents to tell me, in tones of some astonishment, that 'John has decided to stay until he is 18.' My role, at this point, was to give re-assurance and encouragement to a parent who had thought that to keep a boy at school until he was 16, when he might have left at 15, was a tremendous step. If a boy decided to leave when it was thought that he should stay, I interviewed the parents usually with success, but these cases have now become quite exceptional. A bigger problem arises when boy and parent want the school career to continue when it seems that he is unlikely to obtain Advanced Level passes (a serious matter when his parents are poor): often the solution adopted is a probationary year in the sixth form.

About 60 per cent of the boys stayed into the sixth form, and the school demanded no minimum number of Ordinary Level passes. Many sixth-formers seemed marginal in ability when they started, including some of the transfers who came at 16 from bilateral schools (see Chapter 3), but many developed well. The difficulty of prophecy, and the need for some humility, is shown by the following incident. A few years ago, a boy's father asked if his son could stay into the sixth form, in spite of a poor Ordinary Level performance. He entered the sixth on probation, and at the end of the year seemed badly out of his depth. His father was grateful for the information, but asked if his son might, nevertheless, try for his Advanced Level. We agreed, and at the end of the year he obtained three Advanced Level passes. It appears that even schoolmasters are not infallible in their judgments and prophecies.

About half the sixth-formers each year aimed to enter careers in Industry (usually scientific), Commerce and the Professions, and these boys needed much help and advice, which involves knowledge of both local firms and of the increasing numbers of companies which now recruit nationally. The University applicant needed, and obtained, a tremendous amount of information and advice on complicated matters like choice of course (What is the difference, Sir, between Bio-Chemistry, Bacteriology and Micro-Biology?), choice of University (shall I put Leeds and not Birmingham as my University of first preference?), financial assistance, how to fill up a form, how to survive an interview. In my experience, sixth-formers have no inhibitions about asking for this help, and in giving it I got to know them better and felt that I was, perhaps, justifying my existence. Sometimes at this point a boy revealed a personal insecurity which needed a different kind of help: others needed advice about a style of haircut (advice, not a royal command!). A revealing incident may be described. A boy came to ask permission to be away from school in order to attend a University interview. He asked many questions about what he was likely to be asked, and then, with hands still firmly stuck in his pockets, he wandered out saying, 'Well, cheerio, Sir!' I called him back and said that, while I had no

objection to his way of saying goodbye or to his informality, perhaps when he was attending his interview there were certain
things he might bear in mind. The interesting thing is that he
was grateful and said, 'You see, Sir, nobody has ever told me that
before.'

A reference to the School Council is perhaps worth while at
this point, not because it played a major part in the life of the
school (see Chapter 3), but because it illustrates the attitude of
the school to the individual. Boys were encouraged to air their
complaints, to bring them out into the open and to have them discussed. The school had its fair share of these 'sea-lawyers', of
argumentative boys who positively enjoyed pointing out how
wrong-headed authority can be: this is often an irritating process, but I feel it to be of some importance that strongly felt
grievances should be expressed, not suppressed. After all, it is
conceivable that the school has not yet achieved an unnatural
condition of perfection, and that the boy may have a good point.
In any case, is it good tactics to drive all this feeling under-
ground?

There are many grammar schools which feel a serious concern
for the first-generation grammar school child—or if we must
express ourselves in class terms, for the working-class child. What
I have described is the way in which one of their number
attempted to face its responsibilities on the social side (other
chapter deal with curriculum and general education): other
schools have worked out their own individual methods, which
arise from the philosophies and personalities of those in charge.
What cannot be sustained is the charge that the grammar school
as such is insensitive to these matters, and that, by its nature, it
cannot deal with them. No doubt there are some grammar
schools, particularly perhaps in residential areas or controlled by
those who are unduly influenced by what they believe to be
'public school' attitudes and standards, which have not yet
organised themselves to meet what appears to them to be a small
part of their problems. These, indeed, may still be highly
'middle-class' institutions. Again, there no doubt survive a
number of girls' schools which maintain a lady-like aura of respectability and an emphasis on the externals of manners and
appearance which provide an uncomfortable environment for
a girl from a very different background. These will be compelled

to move with the times and are open to the charge of insensitivity and a lack of imagination. It cannot be maintained, however, that even the majority of grammar schools can be so condemned. The myth that the grammar school is static and unchanging may comfort its enemies, but if they believe it they are out of date and out of touch with reality.

Reviewing 'Education and the Working Class' in *The Observer* (11th February 1962), Richard Hoggart referred to the middle-class values which are properly handed on by the grammar school to its pupils. Among these he mentioned 'the capacity for rational and dispassionate reflection, the free play of mind, the literate and civilised qualities'. What he deplored was that these values 'are often rather meanly exclusive, are too much concerned with a surface "style" and "niceness", with small snobbery and narrow gentility'. In so far as this is true, the grammar school is properly to be criticised. It is my contention that the great majority of these schools have already escaped, or are engaged in escaping, from this kind of attitude, and that there is plenty of evidence to show that a rapidly increasing number of working-class children are enjoying happy and fruitful careers within their walls. As that perceptive and critical observer of the grammar school, Frances Stevens, has well said in her book *The Living Tradition* (p. 258) 'a common interest in the world of the mind can resolve the tension of social differences; can set people free to observe them with detachment and even sometimes with pleasure. Grammar school boys and girls, taking a greater strain than those in either public or modern schools, are a true bridge between the two worlds.'

# 3

# *Curriculum and Teaching Methods*

ALTHOUGH EXTERNAL examinations control, to a large extent, the content of the subjects which make up the curriculum of the grammar school, an individual school retains a considerable degree of freedom in deciding which subjects it teaches at a given point in a pupil's progress through the school. Certain subjects are, of course, basic: English, Mathematics, a foreign language (usually French), Science (with great variation as to the amount and degree of division into specialised sciences), Physical Education (covering work in the gymnasium and games) and Religious Education will normally be found in the timetable of children up to the age of 16, although a few may discard the language. History and Geography, either together or as alternatives, are usually regarded as essential, and Music, Art and the boys' and girls' crafts appear at some point. Most schools will allow at least some of their pupils to start Latin, though they may differ as to the timing of this, and at least some introduce a third language in the third or fourth year. The schools which teach either three languages or three separate sciences to their pupils in the main school, that is below the sixth form, must inevitably leave something out to make room for them: the arts and crafts are usually the first victims in boys' schools, to be followed by History or Geography, and in a few sad cases by both.

This draws attention to the first great difficulty which confronts the maker of timetables, the utter impossibility of including everything he feels is educationally valuable. If we think in terms of a week consisting of 35 periods, and remember that at least three of these must be devoted to Physical Education and one to

36

Religious Education, the remaining 31 periods are quite inadequate to meet the demands on them. English, Mathematics and the foreign language will, very properly, expect 15 of these, and the needs of Science, History, Geography, Music, Art, Craft have to be met from the remainder. Almost all boys' schools, and many girls' schools, think it important that two or three separate sciences should be taught at least from the age of 14, which will account for from 8 to 11 periods, and about the same number will disappear if two additional languages are taught. It can be seen, then, how easy it is to embark on an unbalanced if not an unhealthily specialised programme, and how tempting it is to leave out Music, Art and the Crafts. Many boys, if not girls, are very conscious of the qualifications for a particular career, and the parent is not unknown who asks why his son should waste time learning History, Latin or Music 'which he does not need'. A school timetable is at best a compromise. The headmaster has to take into account the actual constitution of his teaching staff, the specialist rooms which are available, his own educational ideas, the traditions of the school, the existence of external examinations, the demands of parents and pupils, of universities and employers. A strong-minded senior subject master may find it possible to play havoc with the balance of the timetable. The existence, locally, of a large number of scientific careers for 16-year-old leavers may compel a considerable emphasis on scientific subjects. If the staff contains one handicraft teacher and there is only one handicraft room, the limit on the amount of handicraft which can be taught is obvious. If the academic reputation of the school is low, the head may feel that, for some years, he must concentrate on bread-and-butter subjects. All these, and many other, considerations hinder him when he tries to produce the ideal timetable.

The second important problem is whether or not to weight the curriculum in a particular direction, at some point in the main school. On the whole, girls' schools have done little of this and have preferred to maintain a common curriculum (with some options) for nearly all their main school pupils. Small schools (for example, those with a two-stream entry) find this question answered for them by their limited number of staff, and co-educational schools, unless very large, are usually in the same position. Larger boys' schools (three or four form entry) find it possible to produce a much more flexible and varied time-table because of their larger staffs, and it is these schools which have produced the biased, and in some cases the specialised time-tables. Closely connected with this has been a strong urge to 'stream' the pupils, that is to arrange them in A, B, C and D forms in accordance with their presumed academic ability. Different streams may have timetables which are weighted in favour of different subjects: if, on top of this, there is a generous provision of optional subjects and the pupils are rearranged into ability sets in some subjects, a highly complex curriculum results and it is possible for individual pupils to have very different time-tables. In principle there is much to be said for a flexible system: some educationalists believe that, ideally, each pupil should have his own personal timetable, and that he should be able to progress at the speed which is most suitable to him in each separate subject. I can see no danger of this state of affairs being realised, but the larger schools are surely right to move as far as they can in this direction.

In one respect, however, they are open to criticism, and this concerns their addiction to 'streaming'. Many schools arrange pupils in ability groups on their performance in the selection examination, even though repeated experience must show them how unreliable this is. By the end of the second year, and some-times earlier, a C or a D form and an A form are clearly sorted out, and apart from a few exceptional cases the pupils will stay in these 'streams' until the end of their fifth year in the school. Thus the process is at work by which the bright, interested boy who entered the school at 11 degenerates into the bored, rather loutish young tough of 15, who seems to be getting very little out of the school. Many of us forget that all children have a vital need to experience success, and it is a great disappointment to pupils who were successful in their primary school when they find that this experience is not repeated in the grammar school. All children cannot be at the top of their form, but these child-ren were judged suitable for an academic type of education at 11, and it is tragic if their abilities are not used and they become discouraged, uninterested and, sometimes, embittered. The school must remember that it creates its own bottom stream, and that if there is a recognisable bottom-stream attitude they have created this as well. Having created this group of potential trouble-makers, the school might at least be expected to take the problem seriously. All too many teachers, however, regard the bottom stream as an infliction and express wonder that many of them ever obtained admission to the school. In reality, this is the biggest challenge to their teaching skill and their maturity as human beings. The weaker pupil, perhaps border-line in ability, needs much understanding and personal help, as well as good teaching. The influence of a good schoolmaster can often save a boy of this kind, rescue him from his own feeling of inadequacy and set him on the way to success, even to success in the sixth form. What a pity that such a salvage operation should so often be necessary! I agree that it is very convenient to teach in one group pupils who are similar in ability, but I am convinced that this convenience should not be purchased at the expense of the children. Any sensitive grammar school head, when regarding with pleasure the intelligent shining faces of his 11-year-old entrants, must be acutely aware of what his school will have made of some of them by the time they are 15.

At High Pavement School, we gave up the practice of streaming in the first year. All boys from the same primary school entered the same first form, otherwise the choice of form for a particular boy was quite fortuitous. At the beginning of the second year Latin started in one form: in order to give the best linguists the chance to start this subject, we put together in this form the boys whose performance in French was best. We thus eliminated one of the original forms, but the other three continued without any grading, and this arrangement was maintained until the end of the third year. At this point, we arranged the boys in four entirely new forms, and streaming and biased courses began. A boy could take one, two or three sciences, one, two or three languages (a few dropped their language outright), History and Geography or one of them. In two forms, boys chose one of the following: Biology, Technical Drawing, Art, Metalwork, Woodwork. One of the forms had collected in it the cleverest boys whose parents said that they would keep them at school until 18, no matter whether they wished to take science or an arts biased course. These boys by-passed Ordinary Level in the subjects which they intended to take at Advanced Level, and it thus became possible to plan a continuous four-year course without the interruption of the irrelevant Ordinary Level exami-

39

nation. Two of the other forms had a science bias, one being expected to make slightly slower progress than the other. The fourth group was in one sense a D form, but it had in it a number of boys of some ability, particularly in the arts subjects, who would probable not stay at school until 18. A complicated series of sets in Mathematics and French cut across the form divisions, so that boys of fairly equal ability in these subjects could be taught together.

I do not pretend that the arrangements which I have just described were in any way ideal. It is no part of the function of a headmaster, when he is newly appointed, to scrap entirely the curriculum which is in existence, if only because some of the pupils have progressed part of the way through it. The best that can be done is gradually to modify it over a period of time. The curriculum of High Pavement School was the result of a long period of gradual development and change. If one were to invent an entirely new system for a new school, one would proceed rather differently.

In 1951 the Ministry of Education published a pamphlet entitled *The Road to the Sixth Form*. Before an unappreciative educational world, the authors of this pamphlet painted a picture of the grammar school as it might be, freed from the tyranny of an external examination at 16, and keeping almost all its pupils until 18. The course in the main school was no longer to be a school-leaving examination, and pupils would only take subjects, at this stage, which were needed for entry to University and the professions: by-passing would be almost complete. The idea was that the schools should be free to plan a continuous course from 11 to 18 with examinations playing their proper part and in no sense dominating the academic life of the school. When the pamphlet first appeared, most grammar school teachers regarded it as hopelessly impracticable, and quite out of touch with the reality they knew. Only a minority of the schools were prepared to attempt to by-pass Ordinary Level. It was clear then, and still is, that many of us love our chains and adhere affectionately to our swaddling clothes. The General Certificate of Education, as it was first conceived, was intended to give the schools the freedom which the School Certificate and Higher School Certificate so seriously limited: unfortunately, most schools set about the task of making the new examinations as such like the old one as they could. Today, at last, with increasing numbers in our sixth forms, and with a rapidly increasing proportion of pupils staying until 18, the way is becoming open for another look at the problem.

In the school I know best, about 60 per cent of the boys stay into the sixth form, and more would like to do so but feel that, academically, they are not quite up to standard. In addition, a number of pupils come into the school and join the sixth form: they 'failed the 11-plus' and have been in G.C.E. courses in bilateral schools. In residential areas of large cities probably as many as 80 per cent of the annual entry will stay at school until 18. Is not the time ripe for a determined campaign to make it clear to all concerned that the normal grammar school course lasts seven years? In any area where the pupil who failed to enter the grammar school at 11 has a realistic chance of later entry (at 13 or 16) his road to the sixth form is open too. It should soon be possible to ask parents, whose children are offered a grammar school place, to sign an agreement to keep them at school until 18 (instead of 16 as at present). Any parent who was unwilling to do this should allow his child to take a G.C.E. course in another type of school. In the Leicestershire scheme it would be very simple to ask parents, who wished their children to go to the grammar school at 14, to keep them there until 18. When, in 1970, all children will stay at school to 16, this change must surely follow. A slightly more generous scheme of maintenance grants, and another modification of the income scale on which these are awarded, should remove financial hardship.

If once it becomes possible to think of a seven-year course as normal, and leaving at 16 as unusual, the curriculum of the school and teaching methods can be reformed. The tendency of the universities to pay less attention to Ordinary Level results, and more to what happens in the sixth form, fits nicely into place, as does the changed attitude of the professional bodies, most of whom are already beginning to prefer candidates with Advanced Level passes. When we have arrived at this position, Ordinary Level need only be taken in the unavoidable cases, and will cease to be a burden on the grammar school.

I have already pointed out that insistent preparation for a mass examination puts a premium on what can easily be examined. Since facts can be more easily examined than ideas and general principles, facts matter most; they can be noted down, learned off by heart, frequently tested and ultimately regurgitated in the appropriate place on the examination paper. Teaching, in certain subjects, can be reduced to the business of filling so many receptacles to the brim with information, as if a school were a petrol station. The need to think, to understand, to be critical is minimised, since the teacher has done most of this by a skilful piece of pre-digestion, and all that the pupil has to do is to repeat second-hand opinions. Is it any wonder that so many pupils are utterly bored, and overworked since the learning process is long and laborious? Their own interests remain unstimulated, they are not trained to work things out for themselves, their will to learn is ruined, and their curiosity killed. When pupils like these encounter mathematical problems, they are mystified and often angry because they have not been able to commit to memory the easy solution and the standard answer. A boy, who is about to enter an Ordinary Level History examination, may well be nothing more than an animated notebook—if animated is the right word. It is perhaps worth remembering that Ordinary Level examinations work on the assumption that at least 40 per cent of the entrants will fail in a particular subject. Thus 40 per cent of this highly selected group, in competition with their fellows, must inevitably fail, and must be expected to do so by those who teach them. The system carries with it an experience of failure for many children: can we not find here part of the cause of the 'C-stream mentality', the contracting-out of the school, and the feelings of frustration which so often produce anti-social behaviour?

The effects of large scale examination on science teaching are worth a particular look since here, at least, one might imagine that enthusiasm and excitement would prevail, and that discovery, experiment and genuine understanding might be essential. However, university scientists, who find it easier to criticise the teaching of science in schools than in universities, have pointed out repeatedly that a great deal is wrong. Mr. Michael Bassey, writing in *The Times Educational Supplement* on 20th April 1962, produced a long list of criticisms. In his view, both Ordinary and Advanced Level syllabuses are overloaded: they present students with long lists of facts which have to be learned. Some of the knowledge they demand is unnecessary and out of date, and could be replaced by much more up-to-date material.

## Curriculum and Teaching Methods

The aim of the teaching, at both levels, seems to him mis-directed, since it appears to aim at producing specialists in the sciences, instead of giving a general scientific education on which can be built an adequate course for those who wish to become scientific specialists. Mr. Bassey's most devastating attack, however, is concerned with the lack of emphasis on scientific method. He states 'I believe that the introduction of science as a method of solving problems is the most needed advance in education today'. One feels inclined to ask what on earth our pupils have been doing in the practical periods which they spend in laboratories.

Obviously, it would be wrong to imply that all grammar school teaching is examination-directed, dull, unimaginative and boring. There are many devoted teachers who teach their pupils to think, in spite of G.C.E., and inspire and stimulate them with a love of their subject which carries them into and beyond the sixth form. Others, through the warmth of their personality and their genuine interest in their pupils as individual persons more than make up for the comparative dullness of their teaching. What cannot be denied is that, in most subjects, Ordinary Level positively encourages standardisation, routine methods and 'talk and chalk', and discourages initiative, individual thought and exciting new methods. Most teachers, therefore, are at their worst when preparing pupils for examinations, and there are far too many, teaching in grammar schools, who have not given teaching methods a thought for years. A few years after they started teaching, they arrived at a method which suited them, partly based on their recollections of the way in which they were taught at school, what they were told when they were trained (if they were!) and on some ideas with which they may fortuitously have come into contact. It is difficult to deny that G.C.E. Ordinary Level has become an incubus and an educational catastrophe, an obstacle in the way of revision of subject syllabuses, an encouragement of lazy and even rank bad teaching. The usefulness it once had has long since disappeared, and the schools have outgrown the need for it.

Once the teacher is freed from the necessity to see that all the pupils in his class progress at approximately the same speed, to concentrate on the fact grind and to emphasise knowledge at the expense of thought, a revolution becomes possible in methods of teaching and in the content and the organisation of the curriculum. His role can change from that of omniscient purveyor of facts, a walking encyclopaedia, into that of leader and guide helping his pupils to solve problems, to find information when they require it and to think things out for themselves. He will be much more concerned with answering, and with helping others to answer, the question WHY? and much less with the question HOW? There will be no need to think in terms of a mass entry at Ordinary Level in six or eight subjects, but he will have every opportunity to concern himself with the individual, his progress and his intellectual growth. Groups of thirty are too large, and for real teaching, new style, classes must be smaller. In fact, a much more flexible organisation is called for. When material has to be given to pupils in order to start them on a new section of their work, it can be done in groups of sixty or even a hundred, and a similar number can see films and television programmes together, and as the new mass teaching techniques are developed this should grow into an important part of the week's activity. When the pupils are actually at work, they should be in sets of about fifteen, with a teacher in charge whose task is to help them to understand, to overcome their difficulties, to learn how to solve problems. In groups of this size, a real personal relationship can be built up between teacher and pupil, and the pupil can be helped to progress at the speed which is suitable for him. The group as a whole can work together as one unit, since the emphasis is no longer on one individual competing against another: if one pupil helps another, the process need no longer be stigmatised as 'cribbing'. Group projects, lasting for a term, could infuse new life into History and Geography: elementary scientific research could be done by the group as a 'team', with each individual taking responsibility for one aspect of the work. The study of a play could lead up to an actual performance in which everyone is involved, and how useful it would be to have a large English room, part stage and part classroom. Where the teacher concerns himself with the development of the individual, he should be able to improve and modify his own teaching methods, and many children, whose careers in the grammar school are not exactly successful, should blossom in the new atmosphere. It cannot be emphasised too much that many grammar school 'failures' are brought about by the rigidity of the school itself,

44

and by its inability to satisfy the needs of a substantial proportion of its pupils. Once remove the stranglehold of the examination, and the need for all this disappears. The potentiality of the grammar school, in its task of handing on the central culture of our society to a new generation, remains substantially untapped: it has a great and glorious future if it manages its affairs aright.

Another feature of the curriculum of the grammar school is its strict division into subject compartments. Single honours courses produce specialists who are only happy when teaching their own subjects. Many heads have had trouble with specialist scientists who are unhappy about General Science: I have met a physicist who was unable to teach General Science because he could not possibly tackle elementary Biology. Heads, who wish to lessen the impact of many specialists on children in their first year, find it hard to persuade teachers to teach even two subjects. Combinations like English, French and Religious Education, or Science and Mathematics, or History and Geography seem reasonable to the administrator, but not so often to the teacher. The newer universities, with their different conceptions of a degree course, may well bring about a substantial change here, and are already influencing the established universities. Granted an influx into the profession of men and women who are happy to teach several subjects, or who have been trained in such a way that subject barriers seem unimportant to them, we may be able to solve this particular problem. Then perhaps we may be in a position to take a second step and try to break down the rigidity of the subjects inside school. The study of man in his environment can surely replace separate History and Geography at least for a time. New conceptions of Mathematics as a language encourage the idea of Mathematics and Physics being taught together at a particular stage. A combination of English Literature and History (for example, the Romantic movement and the French and Industrial Revolutions) is possible and fruitful. English and French language could help each other in combination, if only because it seems a pity that the necessary grammar should be taught twice over, much to the confusion of some children who know about the genitive case in French but cannot recognise it in English.

As 'the Road to the Sixth Form' pointed out, there is no need for all subjects to be taught continuously. Subjects like foreign languages, Mathematics, an individual science need to be taught continuously once they have been started, since a particular skill is gradually being built up and mastery of one part of the subject leads on to further progress: the pamphlet calls these 'linear' subjects. Others like History, Geography, Art, Music can be taught for a time, dropped and resumed, and more obviously lend themselves to work in groups, concentration on particular topics, and the project approach. A timetable planner might then feel it wise to stop the study of History, for example after an introductory course, and resume it, with a greater allocation of time, at a stage in a pupil's development at which he is mature enough to think about some of the problems of man in society. He might, too, take advantage of the younger pupil's ability to acquire knowledge quickly, while enjoying the process, by concentrating more time on the linear subjects in which there is a considerable amount of learning to be done. Flexibility in the timetable becomes possible when individual development becomes more important than group progress at a uniform rate.

I have indicated, earlier in this chapter, that Arts and Crafts are frequently forced out of the timetable, and it would be a fair generalisation that most boys' grammar schools, at least, underestimate their importance. These, however, are the creative subjects, and, if they are left out, where in the timetable do we pay attention to the emotional education of our pupils? (and if the answer is given that it is in the literature periods, do we have enough of them, and do we even use properly the time which we have?). Every school has an obligation to give its pupils the opportunity to develop the artistic abilities and interests they possess, to start them off on this particular line if they appear to have none, to help them to learn to use their hands and to experience the joy of making something by their own efforts. If our commercial society offers little to the teenager which will do these things for him, if, on the other hand, it provides him with innumerable examples of what is shoddy, vulgar and in bad taste, where else can he turn if the school does not help him? Many purveyors of mass entertainment insist that they give the public what the public wants, though their evidence for this assertion is not easy to find; at least the schools might be expected to train their pupils to want material of a better quality.

Most pupils are responsive to music in some form or another. A good music teacher, given adequate time and equipment and starting with the existing tastes of his pupils, can help them to develop an interest which becomes better informed and increasingly subtle, and which may last for a life time. Good teaching in the visual arts, besides helping the artistic gifts of the pupils to grow, can make them use their eyes really to see their surroundings and to respond fully to any beauty which there may be around them: it can also make them conscious of the depressing ugliness of much that makes up their environment. Can any boy, who has been trained by a gifted teacher of woodwork, remain satisfied with the poor craftsmanship demonstrated in much of the furniture which the shops will try to sell him when he sets up a house for his wife and himself? The influence of a gradually improving standard of taste in furniture, curtain materials and carpets can be seen in many shops: we hope that the efforts of schools may cause this improvement to come more quickly. Perhaps I should repeat that all this can be brought about without any attempt at an imposition of what seems to the pupil an arbitrary good taste. He learns, by a proper appreciation of the work of a master of his art or craft, and, by his own efforts, when an object—be it picture, play, sonata or chair—is well-made and beautiful. The creative abilities of many boys and girls remain substantially under-developed. A deep satisfaction can be obtained from painting a picture, writing a poem, modelling in clay, making something in wood or metal, a satisfaction which has great therapeutic value. The conquest of the material, the judgment of the finished product by one's own standards, the feeling that one has created something, can more than make up for failures or disappointments in the academic sphere and in other activities, and can generate self-reliance and poise.

It is no part of my intention to make a detailed study of all the subjects of the curriculum. Since I am myself a historian I shall discuss that subject: in addition I refer briefly to some others, but cannot regard myself as competent to go deeply into them all. Nor does the fact that I shall not discuss Physical Education, for example, imply that I do not regard it as being important.

I hope that I have already indicated my belief that History

47

as a grammar school subject is largely ruined by an external examination at 16. In the early years in the school, a not too detailed exploration of our country's history and of its place in European history is suitable. but it should certainly not be a plodding attempt to cover the whole of the ground. The legal reforms of Henry II, the Cabal, Henry VIII's wives and Ethelred the Unready need have no place. Instead, the emphasis should be on social and economic history, with only a political framework, and at intervals some attention to the growth of the British system of government. Projects, pieces of individual research, the starting off and development of hobbies and interests, like architecture and heraldry, can all be used to stimulate interest and to turn a dead parade of puppets into a lively glimpse of real people actually engaged in living and working. As the child develops into the adolescent, he surely needs, more than anything else, the historical background of the recent past, which will enable him to see his country in its world context at the present time. Events in Asia and Africa, the change from Empire to Commonwealth, the Communist revolutions in Russia and China, the growth of the United Nations and of other world institutions, these are the subjects which should occupy most of the time at this stage: British history will be confined largely to tracing the development of the modern industrial democratic state. Since most of this is difficult to examine externally, I am more than reconciled to the idea that historians should abandon Ordinary Level. Perhaps the most shocking accusation which can be brought against History, as it is often taught in the fourth and fifth years, is that it is boring and irrelevant to the needs of the pupils.

The task of the English teacher in the maintained grammar school is a very difficult one. He is expected to send into a not very sympathetic world pupils who can write and speak their own language accurately and clearly, and he may certainly be expected to be criticised if they cannot. He must persuade them to read widely, and must develop in them a taste for good literature and the capacity to distinguish between what is ephemeral and what is lasting. As a background to all this, he will find that his pupils have access to a tremendous variety of easy pleasures and immediately attractive entertainment. Many of them ask why spend three hours watching a performance of a play by

Shakespeare, written in a language which you find it difficult to understand, when there are so many exciting alternatives? In one-third of the time you can transport yourself out of the dullness of everyday life into an effortless world of thrills and 'kicks' —whether it be through the medium of television, or the jazz club and the dance floor, or even the adventures of James Bond. The truth is that only a minority of the population read for pleasure. Some read because they must face an examination or acquire necessary information or because they have an idle moment: others hardly read at all.

A child who comes from a home which possesses no books, and which hardly sees any apart from those involved in the child's homework, needs a great deal of encouragement before he develops a taste for reading as a hobby. He needs from his English teacher a carefully graduated course in reading, leaning heavily on interest and starting from the point already reached by the pupil (however little advanced it may be) and not at the place where the teacher would like him to be. A detailed study of anything which could be called a set book is entirely out of place until fairly late in a school career. When Shakespeare's plays are introduced they should be acted, not read. Throughout, the attempt should be made to involve the pupil in experiences which seem to him relevant and real. It need hardly be said that this requires great skill and understanding from the teacher, and much tact and perseverance as well. English Literature periods should not lightly be handed over to the efforts of the untried amateur, in order to fill a difficult hole in the timetable. It is the privilege of the English teacher to initiate his pupils into the élite culture: much depends upon the degree of success which he achieves.

To place English Language and English Literature in separate compartments is to arouse the wrath of any progressive English teacher. Any apparent separation here occurs purely for convenience in discussion. An educated man or woman must obviously have acquired a comfortable mastery of the written and spoken word; inarticulateness, in either or both of these respects is not only a handicap in study, in a career and in society, it probably implies a restriction of thought processes and an obstacle in the way of deeper understanding. A child who comes from a verbally inhibited home, where emotions are more often experienced than described or discussed and where vocabulary is limited and abstract thought unusual, is handicapped, indeed, in the highly verbal world of the grammar school. How is he to acquire the capacity to use abstractions, to think in general principles, to speak and write in a highly differentiated and personal manner which he will need if he is to make a success of his academic career? Not nearly enough serious thought has been given, anywhere in the schools, to the solution of this problem, and yet here it is that the English teacher faces his greatest task. There is a real need for a series of enquiries and experiments in this field to include some of the good work which is being done and to help the practising teacher. As part of the approach must certainly come a much greater emphasis on the spoken word. Many children have to be encouraged, first of all, to be able to speak in a group: then they have to learn to express their thoughts and to discuss them with others, and only when they have managed this can much attention be given to accuracy and lucidity. As much work as possible, in all subjects, should be tackled on a discussion basis, and there must be speech competitions of various sorts. Side by side with this a similar process has to be gone through on paper. Formal essays should not appear until late in the course, and written work should have a purpose and a point which is apparent to the pupil.

The reward of the teacher comes when he sees his pupil at last break through, enjoying using words, suffering from a rush of words to the head, becoming a spendthrift and positively wasting words. When this stage has been reached, the boy or girl can develop his or her mental powers and can grow into a mature and fully educated person. Happy is the child to whom all this, through nature or nurture, comes easily: his teacher has the pleasant task of providing the stimulus and the opportunity.

Perhaps the most encouraging development in the field of the curriculum is the beginning of a serious attempt at a radical rethinking of Ordinary and Advanced Level syllabuses in Mathematics, which, when linked with the changes which are taking place in Teachers Training Colleges and primary schools, give real hope that this subject will soon cease to blight the lives of many intelligent children. A substantial proportion of the children who enter the grammar school at 11 come already convinced that Arithmetic and therefore Mathematics is beyond them.

## Curriculum and Teaching Methods

Inside the grammar school, the same process of mystification continues. Many pupils regard Mathematics as a sort of black magic which sometimes works and then, unaccountably, fails the sorcerer's inadequate apprentice. Two important experiments, one centred in Southampton and another in the Midlands, are at work: new courses based upon newly devised syllabuses are being worked out with textbooks and special examination papers at Ordinary and Advanced Level in G.C.E. We are promised an approach which should invigorate and excite the average pupil, without endangering the progress of the most ambitious school mathematician. All that the amateur spectator can do is to applaud these efforts, and pray for a rapid and successful conclusion to these projects. Surely, then, the grammar schools, accused as they are of an obsession with static traditions, will fall over themselves to join in the reform movement. Once the tide of reform is flowing freely, one hopes that syllabuses and examinations will be under constant revision, as mathematical conceptions and techniques develop in the future. It would be unfortunate if a new orthodoxy were to replace the old.

For many years now there have been complaints that the applied sciences are not getting their fair share of the ablest boys who take Science and Mathematics at Advanced Level, together with a quite different complaint from the girls' schools that more girls would be willing to interest themselves in engineering if there were demands for them. A pupil who has achieved considerable success in a pure science at school is often unwilling to change to an applied science: he may feel uncertain about what he is committing himself to, and in any case he is vitally interested in a subject at which he excels. The suggestion is often made that the grammar schools are largely responsible for this unwillingness to change, since they are staffed by pure scientists and those who give advice about careers are often out of touch with the facts of modern industry. There may still be some truth in this, but far more often school staffs are very conscious of the opportunities which exist in industry (a glance at the pages of certain important newspapers is very convincing), but they are not always able to convince a boy that he should make this change, even if their own training allows them to think that they should. Sixth-formers and their parents may ask for and receive a great deal of advice, but they are not compelled to take it: it is not the careers adviser who makes the final decision about a boy's career, nor should it be. (See Chapter 8 for a fuller discussion of this question.)

In order to try to do something to meet this difficulty, High Pavement School began an experimental course in Engineering in the Sixth Form in 1954. The boys took Advanced Level in Mathematics (Pure and Applied), Physics and Technical Drawing and attended Nottingham Technical College for half a day each week, where they took S.3 courses in Applied Mechanics and Heat Engines. With the warm and friendly co-operation of the college, this course has continued up to the present, and has been responsible for producing many engineers at varying levels (some with a degree, some a Diploma in Technology, others with Higher National Diploma or Higher National Certificate). Almost more important, it faced every boy who entered the sixth form to take science with the need to make a choice between pure and applied science. Many boys, who have chosen Mathematics, Physics and Chemistry at this stage, have switched quite happily to technology when applying for a place at University or even at a College of Advanced Technology: for them applied science is nothing rare or exotic, many of their friends have already taken the plunge. Since this course started, a number of grammar schools have tackled the problem in different ways, and there now exist quite a number of schools which have developed technical courses in their sixth forms. It seems to many of us that the distinction between academic and technical education is unreal and unhelpful, more particularly at sixth form level. What most sixth-formers need is the presence of Mathematics and Physics teachers, with some industrial experience, who can prevent these subjects from retaining their abstruse academic flavour by looking at them with the eye of one who has seen their practical application. In my own view, in addition, schools might do well to develop Advanced Level courses in Applied Physics or Engineering Physics, and persuade more examining bodies to set papers: if a pupil had to choose between academic and applied Physics this again would stimulate him to think about his own interests, abilities and future career and would drive him to make a positive choice. Courses of the 'applied' type would be a great help to the pupil who has the 'practical' type of ability—the doer rather than the thinker—the intelligent boy who comes to an understanding of theory through practice, and who is not necessarily less intelligent than one to whom abstract thought comes more easily.

A policy statement, issued by the Committee of the Science Masters Association in 1957, asserted that the effects of science on human life have now become so important that it is impossible to count a person cultured, in the sense that he can take part fully in the life of his time, unless he can understand these effects and the science which produced them. For this reason then, the schools must present science to all pupils as part of our common cultural and humanistic heritage, and in addition the grammar school must continue to provide a preliminary vocational training for the minority who wish to become professional scientists and technologists. Few would deny the truth of these statements. How, then, are they to be applied in practice? The Science Masters Association would like all schools to follow the same course in science up to Ordinary Level, and this course should cover Physics, Chemistry and Biology. The depth to which the study is taken should depend on the ability of the pupils and not on the subjects in which they intend to specialise later. Specialisation in either arts or science should be equally available to every pupil on entering the sixth form. Here I feel that the Science Masters are claiming too much: I cannot see why all children should follow the same course or why boys who are very keen on the sciences should not be allowed to spend a greater proportion of their time on them from about the age of 14. If all pupils are given a good grounding in science in their first three years, a boy who has taken General Science in his fourth and fifth years can still study science in the sixth form.

I agree with the second and third recommendations of the Association, namely that all pupils should study science in the sixth form as a humanistic and cultural subject, and that Advanced Level science subjects should have a reduced factual content. I wish, indeed, that the revised Advanced Level syllabuses,[1] suggested by the Association, had, in fact, been reduced in width in order to clear out of the way a considerable amount of the factual content: then there would have been enough time for a more experimental approach and a concentration on

[1] See Appendix 3.

study in depth. Even the most intelligent subject syllabuses are dangerous, if they occupy too much of the sixth-former's time. I cannot agree that traditional methods are likely to bring about what the science masters state as the first aim of science teaching, 'to lead pupils to observe, and to solve problems by controlled experiments, to draw conclusions from observations, and to appreciate the systematic laws and principles of science'.

It is gratifying to report that the Nuffield Foundation has initiated a fundamental research project which is expected to produce new science syllabuses and to revolutionise school science.[1] Account is being taken of radical changes in content and teaching methods in other countries, including notably modern American experiments in the teaching of Physics. All available teaching aids and new teaching techniques, together with newly written textbooks, are to be integrated in a comprehensive scheme. My only regret is to learn that, even here, there is a danger that no proper regard will be paid to the needs of the applied sciences and of the more practical type of pupil.

Existing teaching methods in Modern Languages are also under fire. It is a matter of simple observation that five years' solid teaching in French does not produce many pupils who can understand or speak the language fluently, and who are confident of their ability to do so. Research in France and in the U.S.A. has led to the belief that there should be a much greater emphasis on oral work and much less on translation. The suggestion is made that oral utterance precedes the written word when a child learns a language, that language is a social activity, and that the only way in which it can become real to a child is for him to use it in real situations. In this view, the first stages of language teaching should be concerned with learning its sound and structure patterns, and these should be really learned until they are reproduced automatically and spontaneously. Translation and grammatical analysis come much later, even though they are easy to test in a mass examination and oral work is much more difficult. Is this the reason why existing teaching methods have become so rigid, and so many teachers are content with a situation in which their pupils have become confused and bored? One can see why, in the past, methods which had been successfully used in teaching Latin and Greek

[1] See Appendix 3.

54

were applied to modern languages: what is not so easy to understand is why so many teachers continue to teach French and German as though they were dead languages. Is it worth asking the tactless question, what is the educational value of learning to translate from a language one partially understands into a language one hardly understands at all? The best teachers, of course, have long stressed oral work, in spite of the fact that only 5 per cent of the marks at Ordinary Level can be obtained from it: is the quickest and simplest change to increase this percentage to twenty or twenty-five? We hear, on every hand, of language laboratories and audio-visual aids. The language laboratory makes possible thoroughness of learning and individual practice at the speed suited to each individual learner, but is very expensive: the putting together of film strip, or film, and tape makes it much easier for the pupil to see and hear his language being used in a real-life situation. There is no doubt that, fairly soon, aids of this sort will be available, in a modified form, for use in the grammar school: at that point, we ought to be on the verge of a revolutionary change[1] in the teaching methods of still another set of subjects. A generation may yet emerge which will show that the Englishman is not congenitally incompetent when speaking a foreign language. Another important step, which is also receiving attention, would be a rapid diffusion of experience in oral examining on a much larger scale: here again the tape recorder may play a significant part.

Before I leave the subject of modern languages, I should perhaps mention the domination of French in the curriculum. In 1960 entries at Ordinary Level were as follows: French 135,578, German 21,806, Italian 634, Spanish 6,213, Russian 514; and at Advanced Level: French 14,627, German 4,183, Italian 267, Spanish 1,168, Russian 141. This great preponderance of French has good traditional, and even educational, reasons behind it, but it can be doubted if it meets present day needs: one is glad to see that a few schools have begun to teach Chinese. There are considerable organisational difficulties in the way of starting different languages with different groups at the age of 11 in the same school. By the time that the pupils are 14, so many changes of form have taken place that it becomes necessary to arrange that all the language teaching in an age-group takes place simul-

[1] See Appendix 3.

taneously. The result is to place a great strain on staffing resources and to make the timetable very inflexible. My last school
started all pupils with French, allowed Latin to about a quarter
of the boys beginning in the second year, in the fourth year
Greek and at least one modern language were introduced for
good linguists (Russian, Italian, Spanish and German were available though not all in the same year), and the better scientists
could start either Russian or German if they wished. This at
least provides another language in the places where it is most
needed, but the predominance of French remains, both in the
timetable and among the staff in the language department.

If we are at all able to look ahead, it becomes obvious that
we can hardly expect the children of the future to be educated
in accordance with the static curriculum and the unchanging
teaching methods which were in vogue about 1950. Technological progress demands and provokes progress in education. We
cannot for ever shut our classroom doors against teaching
machines, programmed learning and a vast amount of teaching
aids, in a pathetic belief in the self-evident superiority of the human teacher, at all times and in all places. While I remain more
certain than ever I was of the unique value of the contact between
human personalities inside and outside the classroom, I am sure
that all perceptive teachers will wish to extend the variety of the
tools and the devices at their command (some may even try
the experiment of applying the techniques of programmed learning to their own teaching). We know already that the teacher
who limits himself to chalk and blackboard, to book, pen, ink
and paper, is losing many opportunities. The enlightened teacher
of A.D. 2,000 will surely look back on 1950 as on an educational
dark age. It is obvious that the new demands which will be
made on human beings, as workers, in their leisure time, as citizens of this country and of the world, must produce rapid changes in the content of the curriculum and teaching methods. We
can hardly march gaily into the 21st century armed with the
mathematics of 1700.

Some of these changes may encourage team teaching and help
us to break with the idea that a class of thirty is appropriate for
most purposes. Some children need individual help or remedial
teaching which they may receive from a particular teacher or
from a machine. Seminar techniques will help small groups of

children to raise and discuss their difficulties, and to go away and solve their own problems. In large groups, there will be a chance for the brilliant lecturer and the use of television and film. All this implies an escape from the sacred principle of 480 square feet for a classroom, the provision in a school of rooms of different sizes, of a language laboratory and a room for teaching machines, of a perfect and instantaneous blackout instead of one that is slow, incomplete and fortuitous. Since future needs in architectural terms are so uncertain, we must accustom ourselves to buildings of a less permanent and expensive character.

As far as specialist work in the sixth form is concerned, for I deal with general studies in another chapter, the picture is considerably brighter than lower down the school, since, at this stage, we are dealing with older boys and girls who ought to be clear about their own intentions and to be on the way towards becoming students. Even here, however, the Advanced Level examination has some important defects. The width of the syllabuses, and the amount of factual information which is required make it difficult for the teacher to digress from the point, and to look out from the boundaries of his subject. He feels under pressure to teach what will be examined, and in my view he generally teaches too much. The risk has to be taken of compelling the pupil to do more thinking and more discovery of information for himself: the teacher should be working towards the role of guide and supervisor. Sixth form work, at its best, involves a close relationship between student and tutor, in which the one helps the other to do his own work. As Plato said: 'Intellectual progress does not take place when the teacher is laying down the law and the pupil is memorising.' The teacher and the pupil must work together to bring the pupil to a rational answer to the question before him. The best methods of education are criticism, question, discussion and debate: learning can only be done by the pupil, assisted by the teacher. R. M. Hutchins, the American educationalist, has said that teaching, like midwifery, is a co-operative art. Particularly for the intending University student, it is important that he should learn to work at this level while at school.

On the arts side, the sixth-former needs a first-class library. The student should have immediate access to texts, books of criticism, biographies, detailed historical and geographical works,

works of scholarship, reference books in great profusion, even if this is an expensive business. While still at school, he has to learn to use a library and the books in it, to discover for himself which books can be 'skimmed' and which must be read thoroughly. The library is the laboratory of the arts student. The scientist needs plenty of time in his laboratory and a great deal of good equipment; ideally he should learn to work alone and solve practical problems for himself. The sixth-former needs a different kind of building from his juniors in the rest of the school. Seminar and discussion rooms, a large library space, numerous laboratories of a special type, common rooms should replace the orthodox classroom. I doubt if either the Ministry of Education or the local education authorities have faced the cost of a large sixth form which is doing its job properly.

What may we expect the curriculum of the future sixth form to be like? A reduction in the content of the individual subject course, and a complete rethinking of some of them, will make possible a redistribution of the sixth-former's time. He should spend rather less than half his time on three A Level subjects (face to face teaching) and the rest should be divided between private study, General Studies and physical education. It should be possible for a student to mix Arts and Science subjects so long as in doing so he does not interfere with his career prospects. On the arts side proper courses should be planned which have some coherence, and a sixth-former should not select three subjects from a list just because he happens to do them well. New subjects should be developed; for example, Sociology, Architecture, Anthropology, Statistics, Electronics. An excellent course might consist of History, Economics and Sociology supported by (unexamined) statistics and a modern language—even though university departments of economics and sociology may object. The principle must surely be established that the education of sixth-formers should not be completely determined by the arbitrary wishes of those who control the next stage of the education of only some of them. One expects, too, that the future will see a greatly increased use in the sixth form of technical aids of all sorts. Sixth-formers, working alone or in groups, can obtain valuable help from programmed learning and teaching machines, from audio-visual aids in general, and a modern language laboratory in particular.

On the science side there is a need for newly devised syllabuses, and one's hope is that the Nuffield experiment is engaged in doing precisely this. Here the emphasis should be rather on intensive than on extensive study: somewhere there must be an element of genuine discovery, and the student must be compelled to face problems which he has to solve. He must, of course, learn to use the fundamental techniques, but there is no need for him to cover the entire groundwork in a particular science. One hopes that the need to learn off by heart great quantities of Chemistry will disappear. Beyond all this, however, the great importance of technology, which will grow even greater in the future, must be recognised, and the built-in prejudice of sixth form scientists against applied science must be eliminated. Applied Physics, Engineering Physics, Mathematics which is really applied, Engineering Drawing, must all be provided, both for the high-flying university candidate and for the student who will be aiming no higher than Higher National Certificate or Diploma. One sees the sixth form scientist, therefore, choosing between courses at different levels, with different objectives and using many different types of equipment in his practical work, and learning how the mind of the scientist works through his own experience. Need it be added that courses in Mathematics will be substantially different from those which have dominated sixth form work so far during this century.

On the arts side, too, there is considerable need for change. The typical History outline period consists of perhaps 200 years, which will be examined at the end of two years when a candidate will probably be asked to answer five questions. It is, of course, a lottery as to which five subjects will turn up, and only the comparatively gentlemanly behaviour of the examiner makes the situation at all possible. The candidate finds himself learning off by heart say a dozen subjects, and offering up a silent prayer that five of these will appear. He may have made a serious study in real depth of the first twenty years of George III, a period which offers an excellent opportunity to study changes in points of view, fashions in interpretation and great historians at work, but the examination question may ask about the Younger Pitt who has only been studied superficially. The emphasis is, therefore, on remembering and the favour of the goddess Fortune. How much better if the candidate were judged on ten pieces of written work, done after serious study and reading during his two years and externally assessed. This process of continuous assessment and external adjudication would put the emphasis on real study and understanding: it could be applied to Geography, Economics, and to literature, English, foreign and classical. What is examined in these subjects is arbitrary at the moment: why not allow the candidate and his teacher to choose, subject to external supervision, those aspects of a given study which he has looked at in depth and has selected for himself. The intending university applicant, by this method, would learn to work by himself, seminar and tutorial would replace lecture, and the role of the teacher would be changed from omniscient encyclopaedia to guide, adviser and friend.

A sixth-former who will be taking one A Level subject, or even none at all—and we must envisage an increase in the number of such pupils in the future—will need courses with a different emphasis. Even in the conventional subjects, freedom from examination control can surely lead to interesting developments with specially devised courses. Newer subjects must also enter the sixth form curriculum. Hele's School, Exeter, already offers, as general courses and not for examination, Computing, Surveying, Electronics, Statistics, Engineering Drawing and Chinese. Add to these Sociology, the Use of English, Public Affairs, a modern language with emphasis on the spoken word and general courses in literature and the arts and crafts, and we have the possibility of an exciting curriculum which should attract the growing boy and girl. As sixth forms increase in size and as authorities increase staffs accordingly, the provision of such courses will become possible. In sixth form colleges and comprehensive schools they seem inevitable.

In attempting some conclusion, it is necessary to emphasise that among much good, devoted and even inspired teaching, which has the happiest influence on those who are fortunate enough to receive it, there is much that is old-fashioned, traditional, humdrum and plain bad. Grammar school teachers acquiesce, with varying degrees of tolerance and reluctance, in the uniformity which a mass-examination system encourages. Many do their best, and with real success, to mitigate its evil effects, many accept it as part of the established order of things and fit in with what they conceive to be its requirements. I am convinced

*Curriculum and Teaching Methods*

that the only real hope of substantial change lies in the gradual removal of Ordinary Level as the objective of teaching in the main school. Once it has gone, a much more flexible organisation of the curriculum will be possible, and many of the new methods which are emerging in a number of subjects will be available. The grammar school has allowed, and is still allowing, itself to be cramped and obstructed in its efforts to introduce the next generation to its cultural inheritance, and the comprehensive school is, to a large extent, imitating it. Granted a reasonable willingness to think afresh, the grammar school has still a most notable part to play in the educational system.

It has to be stated, with emphasis, that it is precisely among those who are new to the grammar school tradition that the worst effects are to be found of the conventional academic curriculum and the stereotyped methods of teaching. The docile, successful pupil often manages to pass through the conditioning process with little apparent harm. When, however, we come to those who find what is offered to them arid and remote, there are many casualties, some of them intelligent boys and girls with real potentiality. These are the pupils who are called lazy by their teachers, who sit dull and unresponsive praying for the lesson to end, whose examination results (frightful criterion!) are disappointing and far below their real ability. For these, the escape from school into 'real life' is awaited with eagerness and it is fortunate for the nation that a considerable number of them transfer with success to part-time further education or a Technical College. Schools have only themselves to blame if pupils prefer to go elsewhere to prepare for A Level, though if the atmosphere is the right one the sixth form offers an invaluable educational experience which is needed particularly by children from under-privileged and under-educated homes.

It is worth asking why so many grammar school teachers write off as hopeless a pupil who fails to respond to their particular methods. Is it not conceivable that it might be the duty of the teacher to change his methods to fit the pupil, instead of expecting the pupil to accommodate himself to the methods? The school is under an obligation to provide a curriculum and methods of teaching which are suitable for the children who are sent to it; even though 80—90 per cent may be able to fit in happily and make creditable progress, the remainder must also

## Curriculum and Teaching Methods

be provided for. Is there not, indeed, a lack of elasticity in the
approach of the average teacher—in grammar, secondary modern
and comprehensive school alike—who convinces himself that
there is a self-evident content and teaching method for a given
subject (of which he is naturally master) and which he is unwilling to modify to any real extent, even when its impact on
children is less than effective? We must look, perhaps, to im-
proved courses in Education in Teacher Training Colleges and
University Departments of Education for a remedy.

To press the matter further—if we are dealing with children
whose experience outside the school does little to help them to
understand, let alone enjoy much of the subject matter which
they meet there (in some cases may be positively hostile to it),
is it sensible either to select material which is as remote as possible from their lives and interests, or to present it in a positively
unattractive manner? If we are choosing a historical period for
sixth form study, do we really think that the Middle Ages is the
most suitable for such boys and girls, even if the teacher is himself a medievalist and if it is easier to win an Oxbridge Open
Scholarship by so doing? When the English teacher is selecting
set books for study, is she right to follow her own interests and
prefer the Metaphysical poets? If a class of middle school boys
finds all poetry, and much of Shakespeare, unreal, stuffy and
fanciful, is there no other English Literature available? There
is surely enough routine dull work which, owing to the nature of
certain subjects, must inevitably be done, without adding un-
necessarily to the burden. Sometimes, one is driven to think that
there are still teachers who feel that there is an educational
value in compelling pupils to study what they dislike. One grants
immediately that the first-class teacher can transcend these difficulties and persuade even the most unlikely children to enjoy
what he himself enjoys, but the fact has to be faced that far too
many children spend far too much of their time in school in
boredom and frustration. It seems almost shocking to say that
this happens in science lessons where one would have thought
that a vital interest was there to be tapped: it is certainly true
in Mathematics and language lessons, in History, English and
Geography. The difficulties in the way of the child from the uncultured home, when he attempts to grasp the cultural opportunities offered by secondary education, tend to be maximised,

62

when it obvious that a sane and rational system would attempt to minimise them.

If then the grammar school, or the comprehensive or secondary modern school, is to succeed in its task of educating to any appreciable extent the children whose need is greatest, there must be a revolution in attitudes inside the classroom, when syllabuses and examinations are planned. It is a tribute to many grammar schools that more and more pupils, from homes of all kinds, are finding happiness and satisfaction in their work and are staying until 18. Newer methods, reformed syllabuses and more enlightened attitudes are spreading, and the leaven is beginning to work. One great encouragement comes from the high quality of so many of the young teachers who are joining the profession: there is a real hope that they may be able to resist the influence of those who are already jaded and defeated. A good grammar school, which has a clear sense of its purpose in the second half of the twentieth century, has still a notable part to play in educating the children of a new class: if it faces this task with sensitivity and understanding, its most valuable contribution to the life of the nation is just beginning to emerge.

# 4

## *General Studies in the Sixth Form*

TO WRITE a chapter with such a title may appear to beg many questions. The implication is that there exists a clear distinction between a specialised education, which concentrates on the development of the mind through studying a few subjects deeply, and a general education which covers a much wider range of human activities less thoroughly. No doubt, if grammar schools were staffed entirely by well-educated specialists, who could see their subjects as part of the spectrum of human knowledge and had the capacity to communicate this attitude to it, it would be unnecessary to write this chapter. We have all met specialists whose teaching is a direct contribution to general education, and from whose lessons no perceptive pupil can emerge without the ability to look outwards from his subject and to see it in a relationship with a greater whole. It would be idle to expect, however, that more than a minority of grammar school teachers could be persons of this calibre. In any case, there are so many pressures on the teacher, from examination syllabuses, University entrance requirements, the demands of professional bodies and other employers, that even the most conscientious among them find themselves forced by a need to compromise between a subject matter and a teaching method which circumstances demand on the one hand, and what they would like to teach and a more exciting method by which they would like to teach it on the other.

The effective domination of the grammar school curriculum by external examinations is an accepted, though a deplorable, fact. It is all very well for secretaries of examination bodies to point out that teachers play a large part in determining examina-

tion syllabuses, that when changes in syllabuses are under discussion it is usually the teachers who resist change and that it is
open to any school to ask for a specially devised paper for an
experimental syllabus. It is natural, though regrettable, for
teachers who have accustomed themselves to a particular syllabus
and the methods required to teach it to prefer the devil they
know to another they have not met. Teachers who have asked for
special syllabuses and papers have not always fared happily:
there is a tendency for examination bodies to be obsessed by
ease of examining, and to turn down suggestions which involve
difficulty and complication. Even when a special paper is set,
problems may arise because of the small number of candidates,
and they are at the mercy of the sometimes arbitrary standards
set by a single examiner. It is fascinating to speculate about the
reception, by one of the larger and more inflexible Examination
Boards, of a proposal by a school that A Level History might be
examined by a process of continuous assessment inside the school,
combined with an external judgment provided by one of the
Board's examiners (see Chapter 3). Beyond all this, however,
there is a deeper problem. Specialist teachers are usually trained
in single honours schools, by methods which aim at the production of research students. As a result, many of them find it
impossible to look at the subject matter of their specialism from
the point of view of one who asks which are the essential facts
and principles which must be taught, and which can be dispensed
with, in the school situation. It is accepted by most people who
think about Advanced Level syllabuses that, in general, they are
too wide and occupy far too much teaching time, because they
contain much unnecessary material, and in some cases need
completely rethinking. Let us take Chemistry, surely one of the
worst examples. Collect together a number of school and University teachers of Chemistry: ask them to revise the Advanced Level
Chemistry syllabus, and what happens? With reluctance they
agree to jettison some of the traditional subject matter, but insist
on replacing it by modern material, and the result is a syllabus
at least as broad as the one they started with. With some trepi-
dation, I state that Advanced Level Chemistry needs to be
cut down by at least one-third, with a concentration on important
principles studied in depth, in order to make room for real practical work, instead of practical exercises all being repeated for

the thousandth time. One of the great disappointments of recent years has been the revision of Advanced Level Physics and Chemistry syllabuses by the Science Masters Association. Many of us had hoped for a considerable reduction in extent, but in vain. Is it foolish to hope that there are some enlightened teachers in these subjects who are capable of distinguishing between the essential and the merely desirable?

Perhaps the remedy for all this, and the problem is by no means confined to the sciences, is to be found in Teachers Training Colleges and University Education Departments. Already, in some of these, a more modern child-centred view of specialist subjects is being inculcated, and the question is being asked what is it important that the pupils should know and should understand? Recent attacks on the content of honours degree courses in Mathematics, very necessary and long-delayed attacks, have led to the suggestion that a different course is needed for intending Mathematics teachers. It is difficult for the uninitiated to understand why a rigorous course of Honours calibre, replanned with the teacher in mind, cannot be established, and this is now being done. In such circumstances University Mathematics departments would be helping to meet the shortage of Mathematics teachers instead of frightening them away.

It has therefore, lamentably, to be accepted that at the present time a great variety of circumstances persuade the grammar school to concentrate its efforts on the sordid business of helping its pupils to pass external examinations, and that this process has a serious effect on what it teaches and the way in which it is taught. Examinations inevitably test what is examinable, and we are all aware that the most precious educational values are often unexaminable. Mass examining, as we know it, is a crude and barbarous method of sitting in judgment, and it leads to a situation in which we undervalue what cannot be examined and overvalue what can. In these circumstances, much thought has properly been given to general studies in schools as an antidote to the worst effects of Ordinary and Advanced Level G.C.E. examinations.

Recent educational enquiries, for example the Crowther and Gulbenkian reports, have criticised the grammar school for both premature and excessive specialisation, and have pointed out that these criticisms are, on the whole, more valid in boys' than in girls' schools. The range of variation in grammar school time-tables is, of course, considerable. The most heavily specialised schools have allowed boys to begin to specialise as scientists or linguists at the age of 12 or 13, and have cut down 'inessential' subjects to a minimum. At the other extreme are schools in which, apart from a few options, all pupils continue the same course up to 16. Other schools have begun biased courses at 14, in which more time is given to the subjects in which the boy will ultimately specialise, without depriving him of contact with a wide range of disciplines. Some schools 'by-pass' the Ordinary Level in subjects which a pupil will take at Advanced Level: others take Ordinary Level a few subjects at a time. Putting on one side the great difficulty of packing every desirable subject into a pupil's individual curriculum, many heads feel that it is desirable for him to be able to spend more time on the subjects he enjoys and can do well, at the stage in his development at which great strides can be made. What we ought all to condemn, however, is a genuine specialisation which prevents a wide educational development at an age which is far too young for any boy to know what are to be his chosen subjects.

Excessive specialisation usually occurs in the sixth form. There are still schools in which the whole of a pupil's timetable, apart from Religious and Physical Education, is concentrated on teaching and private study in three or four specialist subjects. Some schools pay lip-service to the idea of general education by including a few perfunctory current affairs periods in the time-table, but quite obviously do not think them important, and it is hardly surprising that their sixth-formers regard them as an interruption to the vital business of preparing for examinations. If a school offers only two General Studies periods per week, the pupils may be forgiven for concluding that this is a matter which need not be regarded seriously. Many heads, who feel genuinely concerned about the position, are acutely aware of the pressure on their pupils of competition for University places, and have felt it safer to allow their subject specialists a great deal of time: any specialist teacher worth his salt can make a good claim for an increased number of periods, and when he gets them is likely to feel that any loss of time is an interference with an established law of nature. Nevertheless, in 1961, 360 headmasters (of maintained grammar, independent, direct grant, comprehensive and technical schools) signed an Agreement to Broaden the Curriculum (commonly known as A.B.C.), by which they pledged themselves, not later than September 1963, to devote one-third of their sixth form timetable to non-specialist studies (apart from Physical Education and private study). In addition, 270 headmasters accepted the agreement in principle, though they felt unable to put it into operation so early.

Many of the heads who signed this agreement did so because they were anxious that the schools themselves should tackle the problem of narrow specialisation because they thought it was right to do so, and not because of the dictation of some outside body, and they also felt that they would strengthen each other by banding together. They did this in no exclusive spirit and were well aware that many schools, who were unwilling to tie themselves down in this way, were nevertheless coping with the problem by their own methods. Perhaps the factor which led directly to the actual agreement was the proposal made by the Director of the Oxford Institute of Education, A. D. C. Peterson, in 1960 for a reform of Advanced Level which would compel candidates to take four Advanced Level subjects, at least one of which should be a science subject in the case of an arts student, or an Arts subject in the case of a scientist. The whole problem was discussed in a series of conferences arranged by the Institute, and many heads felt that they could not return, like exhausted volcanoes, to their schools and continue exactly as before. Although there was not much support for Peterson's proposal, his initiative stimulated a different solution by compelling real thought. It is now clear that a large number of schools have begun to take general studies seriously, though many still lag behind.

There is no reason to imagine that general studies should be confined to the sixth form. Speaking as a historian, I have long been conscious of the devastating effects of Ordinary Level on my subject. At a time when the pupil has become mature enough to think about, and understand, many of the important political, international, economic and sociological problems of the day, he tends to waste his time in learning great quantities of historical fact solely that he may be examined on them. A good teacher can make sure that these issues are not overlooked, but it seems to me much better to abandon Ordinary Level History and to concentrate instead on the business of preparing pupils, some of whom will leave at 16, to play their part as thoughtful and instructed citizens of a complicated modern world. Similarly, in the case of English Literature, it seems to me wrong to confine the books which are to be studied to the least objectionable of those set in a given year. A two-year course on literature, designed to attract the interest and develop the taste of the pupils, seems to me to be infinitely preferable. This should give time for a less-detailed study of plays, novels and poetry chosen from the 'classics' and from the work of men and women who are writing today. It is quite shocking for a boy to leave school at 16 determined never to have anything to do with Shakespeare again, and we might at least begin early to combat the notion that the only work which needs to be taken seriously is that which is done in preparation for for an external examination. One can easily see, therefore, an area of study in the fourth and fifth years, combining English Literature, History and Religious Education, which is not examined and may be regarded as the forerunner of general studies in the sixth form.

When we turn to the sixth form, we have to bear in mind that, in most schools, this is divided firmly into Arts and Science sides. Unless there is a well-devised general studies course (or an arrangement by which each pupil is compelled to take a subsidiary subject from the other discipline), there is a real danger that the arts student may leave school with no informed knowledge of the importance of science today, and that the scientist may have closed his mind to the arts and the humanities. Here at once there is a serious challenge to those who are planning sixth form timetables. Beyond this, too, we have to remember that many sixth-formers are first generation children. Some of them come from homes which are themselves 'uncultured', have few books apart from those which the pupil brings home from school and may make little use of the public library. Inside their walls, the boy is unlikely to have contact with good music, with the visual arts and with intelligent conversation about serious matters. It has already been suggested that some parents and pupils regard a sixth form education solely as a means to secure a better paid and a better job, and, indeed, who can blame them, since they have not been brought up in the tradition of learning for its own sake. The pressure to do well academically is particularly strong on a boy from a home like this: he has to justify staying on at school by real success. The school has the task of attempting to give a more mature view, especially to those of its students who intend to continue their studies at University. For all these reasons then, any school which fails to take seriously the general education of its sixth-formers is a thoroughly bad school, no matter how excellent its examination results may be, no matter how brilliant the achievements of its 1st XI.

The school has to act in place of the home in many cases, and if we believe that the most important criticism which can be brought against radio and television, cinema and popular Press is that they fail to stimulate and inspire men and women to an interest in what is true, lovely and of good report, we are under an obligation to provide the stimulus and the inspiration inside the school. The arts student may, perhaps, suffer more from surrounding circumstances than the scientist, at least as far as his own studies are concerned. The very nature of the arts subjects demands a sensitivity of mind and a feeling for expression, a lively imagination and an interest in ideas which come from a reading which is both wide and deep and from a stimulating background. The attitude of mind, and the approach to his studies, which are produced in the pupil by his own particular circumstances may make all the difference between success and failure.

Few would disagree with the statement that we should devise a sixth form course that gives both width and depth. Inside their chosen subjects, the pupils must study rigorously and at considerable depth, but the course as a whole must give coherence and perspective to their education: they should see their Physics or their Geography as part of a large whole. Further, should they not go some way towards understanding that the scientist and the creative artist, the craftsman and the philosopher, the religious man and the mathematician each has a different mode of thought which is valid for him, and that no one can say that any of these approaches is better or worse than any other?

Different schools have, very properly, worked out general studies courses[1] for themselves, bearing in mind the particular contribution which can be offered by individual members of

[1] For the work of the General Studies Association, see Appendix 2.

staff. Some schools ask their pupils to take a subsidiary academic subject from the contrary discipline to the one on which they are concentrating. Thus a scientist may study an additional foreign language or English Literature, and an Arts pupil Statistics or the history of science. A number of schools arrange their courses around a list of topics, contributed by teachers from the different departments selecting material which is expected to have a stimulating and inspiring effect when studied in considerable depth. Some schools take social studies as the basis of the course: others give it a philosophical bias. Many different scientific topics are introduced both for the benefit of the arts students and also for the scientists, who often themselves feel that A Level syllabuses at one and the same time narrow the range of their work and prevent them from acquiring a real understanding of some fundamental scientific principles. For example, it seems unfortunate that many sixth form scientists are deprived of the opportunity to study Biology, and in particular Evolution and Heredity.

A school which appears to have a particularly exciting general studies course is Hele's School, Exeter, and I am indebted to its headmaster for permission to describe it in some detail. Here, all sixth-formers undergo a course in Philosophy, Religion and Ethics, and in addition there are three sets of optional subjects, from each of which a topic must be chosen. The first set consists of languages—Russian, German, Italian, Spanish and Chinese (with the hope of Modern Arabic to follow). The second is scientific, and includes computing, surveying, electronics, the history and philosophy of science, statistics and engineering drawing. The third is practical and consists of woodwork, metalwork, engineering workshop practice, art and music. The course is a conscious attempt to meet the needs of the nineteen-seventies and after, and obviously anticipates scientific and commercial developments not only in this country but in other parts of the world. This school also has a particular concern for the sixth-formers who appear to be only average academically, but who are 'doers' rather than thinkers, whose thinking grows from their practical understanding. There are no doubt scores of other schools which are showing great initiative in this field and are developing new ideas and approaches.

At High Pavement School we experimented with a general studies course and did not provide each boy with a subsidiary subject which would give him experience of a different line of study. We felt that the boys who came to us had many varied needs, all of which we must try to meet, and that a positive attempt at an integrated course of general studies does this best. In the past, the school once tried a foreign language course for scientists, in which they were expected to strengthen the language in which they had passed at Ordinary Level. In fact, after some time, we decided that this had degenerated into a mere holding operation, and that the interest of the boys was not really engaged. On the other hand, to start a new foreign language at this stage did not seem profitable, since only some of the scientists seemed good enough linguists to make this worth while. The school has now made it possible for the better scientists to start Russian or German in their fourth year, if they wish to do so.

The elements which make up a general studies course vary much from school to school, and they are chosen because they seem best to fit the needs of the pupils and are within the teaching resources of the staff. If any part of the course is to be a success, the teachers must be able to communicate their enthusiasm and their belief in the significance of what they are doing: the best possible teachers are needed. The danger must be avoided that the course may appear to consist of unrelated bits and pieces. At High Pavement School, we gradually arrived at a basic course which aimed at avoiding this. Arts and Science boys were mixed together in groups, for three periods each week, for a development of civilisation course. Civilisation was here interpreted very broadly, and we included the history of Science, the Arts, Religion, political, social, economic and international developments, the significance of Classical Greece, of the Renaissance, and of the French, American and Russian revolutions. Two teams of masters, including always a scientist and a historian, with teachers of English, Classics or Geography in addition, took charge of the work. Inevitably, a course of this sort must be selective: no attempt was made to give a complete historical background, but the topics which were attempted were, one hoped, dealt with thoroughly. Suitable books, many of them paperbacks, were taken into the periods for borrowing by the boys, who were expected to write two essays a term. During the lesson, every attempt was made to persuade boys to join in discussion, by emphasising the important controversies. As occasion offered, and it frequently did, the course was interrupted and contemporary crises discussed.

In the second year of this course, we largely abandoned the historical treatment and were working towards a topical approach. We were still not satisfied that the sixth-formers themselves were sufficiently engaged in what was taking place: there was too much passive listening. Any experienced schoolmaster must be well aware of the capacity of a pupil to look intelligent while allowing his mind to drift happily away on his own more absorbing thoughts. We therefore introduced a new approach to the topics in the second year. During an experimental year, upper sixth was divided into about five groups of about fifteen Arts and Science students. In turn, each group devoted twelve periods to each of ten topics. In that time they were given a quick survey of the subject, selected a particular aspect of it which interested them, read about it and wrote a short essay. When there was time, some of these pieces of written work were read aloud to the whole group and there was a general discussion. In this way we hoped that the boys would participate more actively, and although the number of topics which were covered in the year were reduced to ten, we felt that they would be covered more thoroughly, and that the real interest of far more of the boys would be aroused. The experiment appeared to be a success, and has continued in operation, though it is possible in future that varying combinations of these different approaches might be tried in other years. The ten subjects which we chose were grouped in two sets of five: the first group was Architecture, the United Nations, the Romantic Movement in Literature, Crime and Punishment, Scientific topics. The second group was Communism, the Mass Media of Communication, Trade Unions, Educational Problems, Scientific topics. These were, of course, selected by individual masters, and were not repeated when another group took over a year later.

Two consecutive periods each week, in which Arts and Science students were grouped together, were spent in discussion of religious, philosophical and ethical problems. What happened in these periods depended very much on the master concerned and the wishes of the boys, and I have discussed in Chapter 6, at some length, the great variety of the matters which arose. What is clear is the need to help boys to think out their own personal

positions and attitudes. I find sixth-formers to be an astonishing
mixture of the cynic and the idealist, the immature adolescent
and the thinking student. They need time in which to grow into
integrated and balanced personalities, and the guidance of a
thoughtful and acceptable grown-up who will help them to move
towards maturity, with no attempt at personal or intellectual
domination. We hoped that these periods gave this sort of help.

A general course in Arts and Crafts occupied two consecutive
weekly periods. There were five options, Art, Drama, Music,
Metalwork and Woodwork. Scientists chose one of these in
each of their sixth form years (though they could only choose
one craft) and the Arts boys joined in their second year. Here
there was a double aim. We hoped that the sixth-former might
learn to express himself in his chosen art or craft, and that at
the same time he might widen and deepen his own appreciation.
Ultimately, perhaps, he would learn to discriminate between
what is shoddy and superficial and what is well-executed and first-
rate: this training in good taste might lead towards a lasting
interest which could give him an ever-deepening happiness.
Many of the sixth-formers enjoyed this part of the general studies
course. They could feel that their own skills and powers of appreciation were growing, and that an interest which they had
already begun to develop, perhaps earlier in their school life,
was beginning to matter more and more to them. If one of the
objects of education is to start off a process which will continue
and grow more important in after-life, we can surely regard this
part of the course as a 'growing-point'. In the sphere of music, it
is most encouraging to find the boys learning to appreciate a
classical symphony, to understand the music of Bartok and to
enquire more closely into the different forms of jazz. In one of
the crafts, we find a boy who comes along with some large extra-
vagant project, which cannot possibly be completed in the time
which he can devote to it. Circumstances conspire to teach him
what he can and cannot do: he learns, for himself, to cut his
plan down to size and to work with (and not against) his materials
and his tools. Here, the school was attempting, in some small way,
to offer an education for leisure—surely an important part of its
task in society which inceasingly provides leisure time for its
citizens to enjoy, or waste.

An additional part of the course, which was intended for

scientists, consisted of two weekly periods which were devoted to English, and aimed to help them to appreciate good writing and speech, and to speak and write well themselves. It is lamentable that scientists and mathematicians find so few opportunities to express themselves in English inside their specialist subjects: as a result, many of them find written work positively irksome, an infliction imposed upon them by an arts headmaster and a wicked world. This part of the course was probably the most difficult to manage successfully. The boys had to be convinced that what they were being asked to do was relevant to their needs, and it was very easy to arouse opposition by what appeared to them an authoritarian approach. Still, some forms of English usage are correct, no matter whether the adolescent boy, who has accustomed himself to slacker modes of expression, likes it or not. The thing has to be done with tact, delicacy, a sense of humour and enough imagination to enable the teacher to look at these matters from the boys' point of view. It certainly helps if they can be induced to see how the work of some modern writers can be vivid, clear and interesting while sacrificing nothing of accuracy. Far too many boys arrive in the sixth form with a limited vocabulary and in a condition of partial inarticulateness. The English department in a grammar school has to work very hard, both in the main school and in the sixth form, to help many boys to overcome the verbal inhibitedness of their home surroundings, which is reinforced by so many of the influences which work on them. This is one of the points at which the culture of the educated man and the culture of the majority may come into acute conflict. Some boys can be convinced that it is worth while to become fully articulate, both in speech and writing, and that this can come about in speech without the adoption of an artificial and socially pretentious accent or vocabulary. The object of the course is achieved if the boys learn to express their thoughts in a language which develops quickly enough to keep pace with the increasing maturity of their thoughts.

A Science course for non-scientists consisted of three periods each week in the first year in the sixth, and one period in the second year. In the first year, the main emphasis was on factual information about recent developments in science, and on scientific ideas which any person may be expected to meet in everyday life. The history of science was covered in the development of civilisation course, in order that it might be available for science as well as for arts students. In addition to demonstations by the master, the boys themselves undertook simple experiments and learned something of the importance of accurate observation, the significance of errors in the handling of apparatus, the danger of having only one experiment and the importance of the interpretation of the results which they obtain. During this year, every opportunity was seized to discuss the methods which the scientist uses, and the relevance and acceptability of the evidence he obtains from his experiments. Each boy was expected to keep his own written record of the work done, and was given some time in school in which to do most of this. He had a number of Pelicans on scientific subjects, and an additional list of recommended paperbacks. No textbook exists which will cover the wide range of subject matter involved, but a collection of relevant books was being built up, and a boy who wished to continue with a particular interest had no difficulty in obtaining access to helpful reading matter. Naturally, many topical questions came up for discussion. Atomic energy leads to a discussion of atomic warfare and its implications. The outbreak of smallpox during the first year of one of the courses made the study of bacteria and viruses more urgent and real.

During the second year of the science course, the emphasis was shifted to a thorough treatment of the philosophical aspects of science. Among other subjects, there were discussions of scientific laws and hypotheses, the question as to how far scientific development rests on the discovery of fresh evidence, and how far on the perception of the implications of existing evidence, and the extent to which man is a chemical machine controlled by hormones. As one expected, at this stage, there followed a far-ranging discussion about the nature of life itself, and a linking-up with the arguments in the religious education periods. It is of great value that materialism, humanism and the science *v.* religion controversy should arise naturally during science lessons. During this second year, a few pieces of written work were asked for, on some of the philosophical aspects of the discussions.

One last weekly period remains to be mentioned. With the first-year sixth, we devoted this to a discussion of important topical problems. This was asked for by the boys in each of a number of years, and the world outside provided plenty of matters which could be discussed with profit. An attempt was made to give a clear, unbiased account of the events or the problem chosen, and this was followed by an opportunity for the boys to express their (usually conflicting) opinions. If there was no controversy, it was usually easy for the teacher to provoke one. In the second-year sixth, the time was occupied by members of staff who, in turn, came before the boys and described, read from and commented on some book which they had found valuable and important. Some of the chosen books were great works of literature: others would be historical, scientific, sociological or biographical books which masters felt were suitable for the purpose. Obviously everything here depends on the capacity of the teacher to communicate his own feeling: the hope was that some of the boys might be induced to read the books, and copies were available.

The accusation is sometimes brought against general studies courses, and has been brought against the one under discussion, that they are superficial. Plainly in some cases this is not true, and a serious study is made of a particular topic: in others, however, it may well be true, and it is a charge of which a school need not necessarily be afraid. A strong case can be made out for offering a rich variety of experiences which are intended to start off the individual sixth-former along some line which appeals to him. If the school is able to arouse an enthusiasm, or help him to develop one which is already aroused, he can safely be left to look after himself when he leaves school. It must be pointed out, again, that the boy or girl of 18 cannot be thought of as a finished product. Nor can it be expected that all sixth-formers will be moved by all the opportunities which are provided for them. A humbler, and more realistic view, is to accept thankfully some progress along the lines (or, indeed, in some cases, along one). In the sphere of general studies, the school's function is not identical with that in an academic subject: different types of courses will be taken to a different depth.

The general studies course at High Pavement School was regarded as experimental. It was changed in one way or another in each of the last three years, and I have no doubt that, as the staff obtain more experience and as they learn from other schools,

77

it will be modified further. Its faults were many, but whatever they were, it was a serious attempt to help the sixth-former towards a greater awareness, a deeper understanding and a wider range of interests and activities, and it occupied nine weekly periods in the case of boys taking arts subjects and ten for scientists.

All boys in the sixth form at the end of their second year took the General Paper (Ordinary Level) set by the Cambridge Examination Syndicate, and at the end of each of the three previous half years a similar paper set by the school. This was done largely to show the boys that the school took General Studies seriously, though the course itself was only distantly related to this paper. There is much controversy today as to whether general studies should be examined. Advanced Level Papers are now set by the Northern Joint Matriculation Board, and an increasing number of schools present candidates for these. Other schools are very doubtful about the whole question of a compulsory examination, even though this may appear to be the simplest way to compel students to regard general studies as an important part of their course. The sceptics are afraid lest a regular Advanced Level General Paper should sooner or later solidify into a fairly routine paper for which pupils will be prepared in exactly the same way as they are prepared for their specialist papers. The hold of examinations on the sixth-former will then be complete, and the schools will again find themselves concentrating on what is examinable rather than on what is educationally valuable. Another disadvantage lies in the tremendous variety of topics which are covered by different schools in these courses, and very properly so: the difficulty of setting an examination which does not limit and inhibit the activities of the school is very great. The strength of a particular school's course will often lie in the teaching of two or three members of staff: if they leave, an entirely different approach may be necessary, and control by an external examination would make this very difficult. In particular, many of the girls' schools with their long history of general courses are, not surprisingly, very wary of such an examination.

In April 1962, a new pattern of University entrance requirements was suggested by a sub-committee of the Committee of Vice-Chancellors, which had been set up for the purpose, but was decisively rejected by the teachers. In addition to a 'course requirement' consisting of least two Advanced Level passes, they suggested that there should be a 'general requirement', which would replace the Ordinary Level passes at present demanded. This test of a candidate's general education would consist of required passes in general papers to be taken not earlier than January in his second year in the sixth form. The general papers would be three in number: first, a paper in the use of English, designed to encourage a serious study of English in the sixth form, to test free composition, comprehension, vocabulary, style and verbal ability, together with accuracy of presentation: second, a general paper (to be set on the assumption that a candidate has already passed at Ordinary Level in either Mathematics or a science subject, together with two or three of the usual arts subjects) which might include questions on general topics for all candidates, questions on literature, history and art, etc., for those taking Advanced Level science, and questions calling for an elementary insight into science and some understanding of simple mathematical processes, of logical problems and modes of quantitative reasoning, presumably for those taking Advanced Level arts subjects; third, a paper in the use of a foreign language. These three papers should be marked pass or fail, and should not be otherwise graded.

The Vice-Chancellors state specifically that they hope to help to bring about a valuable, educational reform, 'an alteration in the balance between general and special studies in the sixth form, placing more weight than hitherto on the former'. They say further that 'the proposed new examination calls for no syllabus or prescribed content of general studies, but, apart from its emphasis on language as a means of communication, leaves the school free to range'. Perhaps it should be added that a number of universities had already decided that they would require a pass in a similar Use of English paper in 1965, and that some universities are in opposition both to the Vice-Chancellor's suggestions and the Use of English paper. London University, in particular, expressed concern at the idea of restricting, by examination, general studies which are only just beginning to grow and should be given more time to develop in freedom. Their alternative suggestion was a strong effort to cut down the content of Advanced Level syllabuses, and to trust the schools to see that adequate attention was given to general education in the sixth form. In order to complete the picture, it is necessary to add that the U.C.C.A. report form for heads of schools, which they complete for all applicants for admission to University, gave an opportunity to show the balance between specialist and minority time, and this in itself was a significant forward step.

I have already expressed above some of my own doubts about compulsory examinations in general studies, though I should not wish in any way to seem unwelcoming to the Vice-Chancellors' initiative, and particularly to the motive which lies behind it. In the case of High Pavement School, if their proposals had been accepted, it would have been necessary to substitute the study of a foreign language for some other material which we had already decided was more valuable to our pupils. Similarly, a school which starts Russian as a second language for its sixth form scientists would almost certainly be compelled, instead, to devote the time to a continued study of the first language, purely for the purpose of the examination. The questions which would be set, on the second general paper, on science for arts candidates would almost certainly come to dictate the topics which were covered by the sixth form : for example, if a considerable number of questions appeared on the history of science, and fewer on modern scientific developments, there would be a corresponding change in balance in sixth form teaching. This would not happen because pupils and teachers are wicked, but because the paper is a hurdle which must be surmounted before a University place can be obtained. All the time, it has to be remembered, too, that the weaker candidate for University entrance has an increased burden to carry. The new proposals will not increase the number of University places, and keen competition will still mean that good marks in specialist subjects will be needed : on top of this, the general papers must be passed.

My own temporary solution would be along the following lines. It seems to me entirely proper that there should be a compulsory paper in the Use of English, if only to get rid of the useless Ordinary Level pass in English Language (though some of the recent experiments do not by any means win the support of the schools, and much further trial and error is required). After that, I think that there should be two alternative ways in which evidence could be given that a satisfactory standard of work in general studies had been achieved. Where the schools wish it, and where examining bodies are prepared to set the papers, pupils should take the general papers based on the Vice-Chancellors' proposals: much experiment has been devoted to the provision of these papers in Manchester, and many schools thoroughly approve of them. The alternative scheme should be one by which any school, which was devoting a given proportion of its time to general studies (and whether or not it is an A.B.C. school is immaterial), could apply to be 'accredited' and allowed to decide internally if a given candidate for University entrance had reached a high enough standard in his general studies. A process of external moderation would be necessary by which the arrangements for general studies in the school would be looked at and samples of written work investigated. There would be no need for a school to hold its own general studies examination if it preferred a process of continuing assessment throughout the course, and this would be an advantage of the scheme. The local University Institute of Education would be the obvious body to take charge of the accrediting and moderation, and one hopes that, after a gradual introduction of the idea, it would not impose an impossible burden upon them. It could, indeed, go much farther and arrange meetings between University and sixth form teachers, at which there would be a discussion of syllabuses and teaching methods. The more that meetings and discussions of this sort are built into the structure of the educational system, the better for both universities and schools. Is it fanciful to hope that experiment on these lines may gradually lead to a situation in which accrediting can be extended to specialist subjects and Advanced Level reduced simply to a qualifying standard? After all, accrediting and external moderation, supplementing internal assessment, are well known in Victoria (Australia) and in the United States, and a different version of the same method is used in many Teachers Training Colleges and University Institutes of Education in this country.

This chapter started with a discussion of the domination of the grammar school by external examinations, and it is no coincidence that it ends on the same note. I should be unhappy to see any steps taken which would rivet the shackles of the examination system still more firmly on the teacher. What we ought to be doing, surely, is to encourage him, by every means in our power, to stand on his own feet, to think out the answer to questions like these; what should properly constitute the liberal education which my pupils need? What can I teach them will contribute to this? What methods are most suitable to help in the personal development of a particular pupil at this stage which he has now reached? How much longer will teachers be satisfied with asking themselves an entirely different question: how best can I get this group of pupils through G.C.E.?

# 5

# *Authority and Freedom in the School*

TRADITIONALLY, THE English grammar school has been organised as a dictatorship, benevolent or otherwise. Once appointed, the headmaster has been supreme. He it was who decided on policy, determined the tone and atmosphere of the school and appointed the staff. He was responsible to his governors for the entire management of the school, but if he was a man of strong personality would find this fact restrained him but little. Today, the situation in the maintained grammar school is considerably different, and it has changed appreciably since the Education Act of 1944. Each school should possess an Instrument of Government which lays down the distribution of the responsibility for the running of the school. In the standard form, the head is responsible to the governors for the curriculum, the organisation of the school and the welfare of the pupils. In many areas, however, governors have little power and provide a façade behind which the Education Committee or even the Director of Education exercise effective control. The head has to bear in mind his responsibility to many different persons, some of them perhaps innocent of any real knowledge of education, or even of the purpose of the school which they help to govern. He is responsible to his governors, to the Education Committee, to the Director of Education, to the Ministry of Education and above all to the parents of his pupils. He has always to remember that the ratepayer is his ultimate master, and that the more sensational Press can be relied upon to call the attention of public opinion to any injudicious statement he may make, to any unfortunate incident in which his pupils may be concerned, or to any

83

decision which can be distorted to look like a serious interference with the liberty of pupil or parent. Apart from this,
the head of a maintained grammar school is free to do what
he likes.

Many heads of schools would welcome the support of an
interested governing body which contained a number of men
and women who had a genuine, not an artificial, interest in the
school and its concerns. Since the Education Committee must
always have full financial control, through its acceptance or re-
jection of estimates of expenditure, there is no reason why it
should provide either the chairman or a majority of the members
of each governing body. Are not members of Education Committees for ever complaining that they have too many meetings?
Each secondary school needs a governing body of its own which
should be made up of a small number of members of the Education Committee, representatives of the parents of pupils in
the school, members of the teaching staff of the school and
members of the general public who have some special knowledge
of educational affairs (for example, a member of a University or
Training College staff). A governing body which is shared between schools can have no reality, and is usually established when
Education Committees are determined to deny governors any real
influence or power. Such proposals as these will no doubt out-
rage the hearts of many local politicians who, while possessing no
particular qualification for membership of a governing body or
even a real interest in educational affairs, enjoy appearing on
Speech Day platforms, appointing heads of schools and feeling
that they are in a position of authority. What a school needs is
a body of men and women who really care about it, are prepared
to devote their time and energy to it and, if necessary, are determined to fight for it.

Inside the school, the head may share his responsibilty as much
or as little as he wishes: as far as governors or Education Committees are concerned, he is the responsible person and this is the
source of his power. Even in what appear to be the most auto-
cratically run institutions, however, the subtle interplay of
personalities and the coming into existence of conventions and
traditions may produce fascinating modifications in this simple
structure of authority. Headmasters, indeed, are not what they
were: the day of the great headmaster, that awe-inspiring figure

whose word was law and who could look into your very soul, has gone—for ever, one hopes.

Most headmasters, indeed most persons who occupy a position of responsibility, will say that they believe in the principle of the delegation of responsibility, though this can be anything from mere lip service to a complete reality. In a school, it is important that one's colleagues should be given responsibility for a particular task and should be expected to get on with it without interference, though if they wish to discuss any matter they should be able to do so. Therefore, heads of subject departments should be given real control over syllabuses, allocation of staff to forms, choice of textbooks and teaching aids, and should be consulted when new appointments are being made to their department. Where senior house masters exist (that is, in a school which uses the house system seriously) they should be able to exercise an effective supervision over the boys in their care, should receive all possible information about them, meet their parents and be consulted when their affairs are under discussion. The deputy headmaster should be given real responsibility for some area of school life—in some schools he takes charge of the junior school or of the administration of school discipline: he will deputise for the head, and will be consulted about matters of policy. Similarly, the careers master, the librarian, the masters in charge of the various games, the master in charge of the timetable, the bursar or administrative assistant where he exists (and why the head of every school of a substantial size is not given such administrative help is a complete mystery) should all be given authority within their own particular sphere, an authority which involves making decisions which may be important in the life of the school. Only when these decisions are likely to have serious repercussions on the outside world is it imperative that the head should be consulted. Most heads of schools find themselves submerged in a sea of detail, have little time to think about educational problems, see what is happening in the school or meet individual pupils: if they do not delegate a great deal, I can see a sad fate in store, at best a stomach ulcer, at worst suicide. Apart from this, a staff room is far happier when twenty of its members have a real stake in the school, and are doing a job which interests them, unhampered by continual interference.

More important than this, it seems to me that the only sensible way in which a school can be run is as a co-operative enterprise between staff and head. All major policy decisions should be made by staff and head in consultation: sometimes this will take place at a full staff meeting, on other occasions by a committee of relevant persons to which responsibility for a particular matter has been given (for example, the organisation of holiday parties or the management of school games). It is, of course, much quicker, simpler and less frustrating for him if the head settles matters alone and issues an imperial edict. It is often possible that more sensible decisions might be arrived at in this way, since the collective will of a group does not always measure up to the intelligence and good sense of its individual members. Situations are not unknown, too, in which individual members of staff have been able to use the loftiest educational principles as a camouflage for their own selfish interests. On the other hand, all important decisions, however arrived at, have to be put into operation by the teaching staff of the school. Since they are responsible men and women they must surely be allowed to play a part in determining a policy which they have to execute. If they are not all fully responsible adults, the only way to make them so is to compel them to face their responsibilities and to grow to them. A head may find, quite often, that he has to be content with an inadequate compromise, but it seems to me essential that he should carry his colleagues with him, even if they act as a brake upon progress. One part of my own experience has been the gradual conversion of a staff, stage by stage, to accept the principle that where a school insists upon compulsory games, senior pupils should be allowed a range of options from which to choose. Important decisions which involve changes in the curriculum must surely be made by the staff concerned, if their wholehearted co-operation is to be secured. An intelligent head realises that he has no monopoly of educational wisdom, and that a democratic and co-operative exercise of authority is infinitely more rewarding than despotism could ever be. New ideas and progressive suggestions may come from many quarters: it must be very exhausting to be the single fountain head of progress. Apparently insoluble problems can be solved by the collective wisdom of a group, and individual masters can be seen to develop in maturity and expertise. A head has, too, a particular responsibility for the progress and development of his young teachers: his advice, guidance, judicious suggestions and even his availability can be a tower of strength to a beginner.

The head must forever be looking, then, towards the outside world and the image of his school which is seen there. Inside the school most of his powers will be delegated or used in co-operation with his colleagues: an authoritarian outlook is out of date at this moment in time, and is out of place in a democratic society. Despotism, inevitably, stems from a lack of faith in others.

Indeed, most schools need much more help on the administrative side. A large school should have a full-time bursar who can relieve the head and staff of much detailed administrative work. There is a need for a housekeeper who can take complete charge of school meals, entertainment of visitors and visiting teams, the provision of tea and coffee at appropriate intervals, and the cleaning staff (though I am well aware that this proposal will cut directly across some School Meals and Caretaking Department empires). A school of 800 pupils needs a full-time librarian and a full-time careers expert. The main job of professional teachers is to teach: their time should not be wasted on jobs which can be done more efficiently by trained experts. The chief tasks of the head are concerned with policy decisions and human relations: there is no danger that he will be under-employed. In addition, he will probably be expected to play an effective part in the life of the neighbourhood, and he must have enough time and energy left to do this.

The foundation of authority as between teacher and pupil, between the mature adult and the immature child, is quite clear. If a teacher gives an order to a pupil, it must be obeyed. 'You will do exercise seventeen for homework' (the implication being, whether you like it or not, because I think you ought). 'You will be silent' (because I say so). 'I cannot run this school on the understanding that you will obey an order only if you happen to feel like it' (to a boy of sixteen). On the other hand, if this represents the total picture of the relations between teacher and pupil there is little chance for the pupils to develop self-reliance, initiative and self-discipline: nor are they likely to grow into adults who are capable of self-government and of active participation in the affairs of a democracy.

## Authority and Freedom in the School

In the adult world, it is necessary to have laws and both officers and courts to enforce them and to punish offenders:
naturally, in the case of immature children there must also be
rules and machinery for their enforcement. In the lives of most
well-intentioned adults, police and courts are of little importance
(unless, indeed, they happen to possess a motor-car): they are
held in reserve. A school ought surely to work in much the same
way. Authority and punishment should be in reserve and orders
should rarely be given, and when they are given they should
appear reasonable to the pupils even if they are not thoroughly
acceptable. If pupils feel that the staff are well-intentioned, liberal
and 'on their side', they will be prepared to acquiesce when
commands seem pointless and unnecessary: in a word, they will
be co-operative. Danger arises when a member of staff is excessively conscious of his authority and appears positively to seek
occasions in which he may be offended, if not outraged. The good
disciplinarian is no authoritarian person whose word is law and
in whose presence none may blink an eyelid: he is rather the
friendly, understanding man with whom all pupils co-operate
happily, and in whose presence no question of 'discipline' ever
arises, on either side.

In theory at least, in a democratic society the laws which are
made represent the will of the majority. In practice, the average
citizen feels somewhat remote from both the legislative and
executive functions: many of our fellow citizens are concerned
about the relations between 'us' and 'them'. If, for example, Her
Majesty's Government decides upon some important new policy
—for example a 'wage-pause'—it is not easily clear that they have
a mandate from the electorate to do this: it certainly looks to
the man in the street that it would require at least the interven-
tion of the devil and all his angels to stop them, before they
are ready to bring the 'pause' to an end. In school, too, in practice, authority often seems to the schoolboy remote, incalculable
and uncontrollable, and there we have no general election
through which the voter can preserve some tenuous control of
the government.

In my last school, however, we had a School Council for more
than fourteen years. This was an advisory body which consisted
of representatives of the different age-groups in the school (with
first-formers present as observers), and a more heavily weighted

88

representation of the sixth forms. There were six staff representatives, and the headmaster and his deputy and the school captain and vice-captains were present *ex officio*. The school captain was chairman, and a boy was elected secretary. The Council discussed and voted on resolutions sent in by the forms, and at question time asked for information. It did not discuss matters connected with the school curriculum. The headmaster had the power to veto the inclusion of a matter on the agenda (a power which was used only three times in fourteen years) and to refuse to accept resolutions which the Council had passed (again this was done only rarely). During its history, the Council made many excellent suggestions (among others, it brought about important changes in school uniform and the organisation of Assembly), and got rid of many things, small and large, which needed attention or reform. Ultimately, of course, the School Council had no authority apart from what I gave it, and some of the pupils felt that its powers were too limited for it to be of much use: it is, however, difficult to see how such a Council could have much more power in a maintained school. From my point of view, the existence of a School Council had many advantages. It offered a partial training in self-government, and at the same time made sure that grievances and difficulties came to light. In general, it functioned with considerable good sense, and it was fascinating to see what happened when a sectional interest attempted to gain some privilege for itself. The boys learnt how to work democratic procedures: they learnt the value of compromise, and even those who were impatient to accomplish a desirable reform in the twinkling of an eye had to learn the limitation of the possible. Boys must feel able to raise their difficulties, secure that these will be considered sympathetically, and they should learn to refuse to accept statements without evidence. Above all, they must know that they can ask for help when they are in trouble, from their form master during their first year and from their house master as they move farther up the school. It is not unknown for boys to approach the headmaster on these occasions. What we were striving to produce was an atmosphere of ordered freedom, in which a boy had no feeling of being regimented even though he could not do exactly what he liked. The object was a gradual development of self-discipline.

It is not surprising that relations between teacher and sixth former should be different from those between teacher and second-former. Intelligent boys of 16 to 19, who have stayed on at school because they wish to do so and not because the law compels, must be treated as young adults. Many are already young men and would be earning large sums of money if they had left school: they have acquired adult habits and it would be ridiculous to treat them like schoolboys. Ideally, the sixth form should be housed in a block which is separate from the rest of the school, with smallish classrooms and discussion rooms, a library of their own and common rooms with a coffee bar and a place to smoke. There should also be parking space for their cars, motor-cycles and scooters. In spite of their varying degrees of maturity and immaturity, they should be regarded as adults until they show clearly that they are not: at that point, their imperfections must be pointed out with some force. Most schools, unfortunately, lack a separate home for the sixth forms, and those who are in these circumstances have to try hard to carry out the policy in inadequate surroundings. Some masters and mistresses find it hard to establish the right relationship with sixth-formers: at one extreme excessive friendliness and inability to keep a reasonable distance, at the other an obsession with personal dignity and a failure to discuss on terms of equality alike lead to difficulty. In the eyes of his staff, a headmaster's worst sin is to fail to support a colleague when he is in a dispute with a pupil: he is in an awkward position when a colleague makes himself ridiculous by his attitude to a sixth-former. For my own part, I wanted a completely frank relationship with a sixth-former: he was perfectly entitled to tell me that he thought me mistaken, so long as he did so politely: naturally, I reserved the right to do the same. Even if he failed in politeness, I had faith in my ability to deal with the situation.

Ideally, of course, there should be no need for a violent transition when a boy enters the sixth form: the change in relations between staff and pupil should come about gradually between 14 and 16. The authoritarian outlook is rarely successful with the adolescent, who must be prepared to accept the authority of both teacher and prefect, but he will be much happier if he can see it as reasonable, well-intentioned and humane. When relations can be put on a personal basis, they are usually more successful: if you are talking to someone who knows you, and whom you know, there is a likelihood of a growth of mutual respect and understanding. This may be difficult in a large school, and there is always the fact of differing attitudes among a large staff. To put the matter at its most moderate, many difficult situations which involve staff and boys ought not to be allowed to arise.

So far, I have largely ignored the existence of the prefect system, that legacy from the public school. Many heads have misgivings about the possibility of reconciling the prefect system with a more democratic school organisation, and it is even possible to find sixth-formers who are unwilling to become prefects. In spite of all this, most grammar schools in fact operate the prefect system, presumably because it appears to give the best opportunity to senior boys to use authority and to learn to take responsibility for others. In certain quarters, it is fashionable to sneer at the very conception of leadership, as if it were not necessary in almost every institution for someone to undertake responsibility. What is most important, surely, is to ask oneself what are the qualifications one looks for in a leader, and what is the nature of the responsibilities which the leader is asked to assume. In a very large sixth form, one of the serious problems is to find responsible jobs for as many people as possible. Apart from positions like games captain, official or committee member of a school society, there is a shortage of what might be described as functional posts. Some schools select library, milk or dinner prefects: others may give a sixth-former the duty of looking after a particular form. In addition to this, it is useful to have prefects with general disciplinary powers, and this is the position in most schools. Now that school prefects are no longer regarded as a sort of Praetorian Guard—or even as the headmaster's secret police—it is possible to see that they keep a sense of proportion about themselves, and there is no need to exaggerate either their importance or their villainy. They can learn to exercise their powers with some concern for the ordinary boy, and may even discover for themselves the limited value of punishment. They may be nominated by the head alone or acting with house masters: they may be elected at a staff meeting, perhaps from a list of boys nominated by the sixth form: sometimes they are elected by the boys themselves. The actual method matters little, if the boys feel that it is fair, that a great deal of trouble is taken, that boys who are not good games players are not excluded and that personal prejudices do not count when selection is being made.

So far, I have been attempting to show that it is perfectly possible for a school which is essentially an authoritarian state, in the sense that final power is concentrated in the hands of one person or a small group of persons, to be democratic in spirit and attitudes and to provide an atmosphere in which pupils can feel both happy and respected as persons.

One last aspect of authority in school, and that perhaps the most important of all, remains to be discussed. Granted that it is the function of the grammar school to hand on to the next generation what is best in our cultural inheritance, a number of questions have to be answered. Who is to decide precisely what is important and valuable enough to be passed on? To what extent is the school to adopt an authoritarian attitude while in the act of transmission? Obviously, when a teacher is dealing with matters of fact he will feel himself entitled to claim that such and such a thing is true and must be accepted without question. He will, no doubt, be prepared to demonstrate or prove the truth of what he is saying on some occasions, but if he is teaching French his pupils must be prepared to accept his state-ment that the French word for 'man' is 'l'homme'. Is he entitled to adopt exactly the same policy when he is dealing with matters of opinion, matters of taste, questions about which there is much dispute in the adult world?

When a pupil comes from a home with low cultural standards, for example where there are few books, where he has no contact with music or the visual arts, where there is no serious attempt at moral training, it has become generally accepted in this country that the school must step in to remedy the deficiencies of the home. Indeed, in my experience, the majority of parents expect the school to do exactly this. I have often had a boy handed to me at 11, almost as if he were a parcel, with the remark, 'Please do your best for him: I can do nothing to help him. You see, I left school at fourteen.' In these circumstances, the school does its best, realising, inevitably, that the result of its activities may be to set up a conflict in the mind of the boy himself: the standards which he meets at school may seem to him to be alarmingly different from the ones he is used to at home. If the school is sensitive to this possibility and is prepared to be sympathetic and understanding, tension of this kind produces few lasting effects, although it may be very uncomfortable for the pupil for some time. In learning to cope with the difficulty, he is developing in maturity, though a good school will surely attempt to minimise the difficulty: one learns adaptability and resourcefulness as part of the process of growing up. I have attempted to deal with the difficulties caused by this conflict of standards at some length in another chapter of this book.

When a pupil arrives at the grammar school at the age of 11, he finds that the school has certain traditions and standards, which are very much influenced by the attitudes of the educated man outside. The school may see it as its duty to communicate the standards described elsewhere as those of the Establishment, or it may prefer those of what I have called the Intelligentsia, depending perhaps on the traditions of the school or the nature of its teaching staff. Most pupils accept the attitudes of the school at first, and to a greater or lesser extent are influenced by them. With many, this influence continues and increases throughout their school career: some boys will accept part and question other parts of the school's outlook. There are a few, too, who become complete rebels against everything the school stands for. Presumably, the head and staff, aided by examining and other bodies, and with some reference to parental wishes, decide what shall be handed on, and having done so proceed to train their pupils, using their best skills, and with their full authority as schoolmasters.

I myself regard it as right to be authoritarian in some matters, but permissive and non-directive in others. I am quite sure that it is wrong to tell lies and right to tell the truth (though I should allow certain exceptions if challenged by my pupils). I am equally sure that King's College Chapel, Cambridge, is a better piece of architecture than the Nottingham Council House. I should be authoritarian when dealing with truth and falsehood, though ready to say why, but I should not be authoritarian when discussing matters of taste in the arts. This is, of course, partly a matter of tactics. I cannot think it wise to convince your audience that you regard them as ignorant philistines, and that you propose to enlighten them whether they like it or not. With senior boys, you can take your horse to the stream, but you

93

cannot compel him to drink. At best, you may, if you are skilful enough, persuade him that water has a pleasant taste. The authoritarian view of culture is unpleasantly condescending, and I have no use for a minority élite which decides what is best for others, and administers the medicine accordingly. In school, there should be a clear statement of your views and of the reasons why you hold them: this should be followed by a discussion, but there must be no implication that you are 'right' and that all right-minded people agree with you. The important thing is that intelligent boys should learn to question, discuss, sort things out for themselves and develop their own tastes and standards, partly as a result of exposure to yours. There should be no attempt at the process of conversion.

How far do I apply this attitude to the religious and moral sphere? I have already said that I am prepared to dogmatise about truthfulness and, I should add, honesty. The consensus of opinion on these matters is quite clear, of all that is best in past or present, in the thought of Christian or Buddhist, in the view of Socrates and also of the scientific humanist. I am not prepared to dogmatise about sexual morality or with regard to relations with parents, though I make my own view completely clear. In addition, I am pretty dogmatic about the important principle which gives to all other human beings equal rights with onself. I am not prepared to be authoritarian about religion, or about belief in Christianity, in the sense that I would state that no intelligent man can possibly be without a religion, or, in this country, that he can avoid being a Christian: I am certainly unwilling to teach, as accepted truths, some of the beliefs which the Agreed Syllabus expects me to teach. Similarly, I should not dream of acting as a propagandist for any particular set of political ideas inside the school. If there are people who feel that my non-directive approach in religious affairs is thoroughly misguided, I invite them to tell me if they would like me to be equally authoritarian in the field of politics. I agree, however, that what one teaches is often coloured by one's strong convictions, in religion and politics alike.

My general position is, then, that it is my duty to transmit to my pupils our cultural heritage, but not in the sense of giving to them a finished, highly polished article of great price which they refuse at their peril. I must help them towards a greater awareness, deeper thought and wider interest. I must open doors for them. I must help them to bring themselves into contact with a wider range of man's activities, and so develop themselves if possible to the point at which they may be able to make their own contribution in the artistic, scientific, religious and other fields. What I should not do is to attempt to impose upon them my own beliefs (no matter how sure I may be that I am right) or my own cultural standards (no matter how superior I may know them to be to theirs—superior in the sense that the B Minor Mass is better than *My Fair Lady*). I must provide them with the knowledge which is required before they can think things out for themselves: facts are sacred and should have their own authority, in education as well as in journalism. Perhaps I should add, too, that I must teach them to live as members of a community, recognising both the rights of their fellow men and the authority of the law.

There is a sense in which it is distasteful to think that one of the main objects of the grammar school is to pass on the cultural inheritance. The 18-year-old who fits neatly into the cultural expectations of the adult world may not so much have finished thinking for himself as not have started. A 'cultured' boy or girl of this age is rather a pitiable object. When he leaves the sixth form, he should be in the middle of an unfinished process: in some respects he may be crude and raw, uneven and unpolished. He should ideally be critical, but he must certainly be developing quickly. He is obviously immature and lacks experience of life and human relations, of political affairs and of the arts, and must be expected to be so. The purpose of the grammar school must not be to produce cultural conformists, but people willing and able to behave as individuals, able to recognise the tremendous debt which they owe to the past while possessing both the capacity and the desire to move on in the future. A school which demands receptivity and is authoritarian in its attitudes and methods needs to think again, or indeed needs to think. A mind which is to all intents and purposes closed is no valuable equipment with which to face the rapid changes of the second half of the twentieth century. In the past cultural progress and development have come from individual persons who have thought things out for themselves, who have felt for themselves and who have been unwilling to fit themselves into

95

accepted and conventional patterns; great innovators like Cézanne, Beethoven, Einstein and Wordsworth.

An attitude which encourages pupils to think things out for themselves is likely to produce much criticism both of the school and of society at large. If pupils are engaged in thinking for themselves they will think some strange, wild and woolly things which authoritarian adults will find subversive and even shocking—this situation is a serious test of the maturity of the adults who have to deal with them. Surely, however, what a sixth-former thinks is of very little importance to anyone except himself: he will change his mind many times as he matures, and the important thing is that he should go on thinking. What the sixth-former does has of course more relevance, and there is often a much less close connection between what he thinks and what he does than he would like to think. Those in authority must have faith and remember the days of their own youth, unless, indeed, they never went through the questioning process and the stage of criticism, and settled down into conventional middle-aged opinions at the ripe age of 17. The cowardly policy in a school is to play for safety and to stifle opinions and criticism in deference to Directors of Education, School Governors and public opinion outside. One of the engaging qualities of the young is their unwillingness to play for safety: their right to refuse to do this must be defended by those who teach them and should know them the best.

I conclude, therefore, that there are real and significant limits to the use of authority in the school. A school exists in order to help personalities to grow: it should offer only the minimum of restrictions which limit growth and must rather provide conditions in which growth is encouraged. The corruption of power is as dangerous in a school as anywhere. A recent book describes the qualities of the mass society as 'uniformity of basic values, standardisation in consumption patterns, and power which is concentrated in a bureaucratic organisation beyond the scope of influence by the individual'. It is interesting that the mass society thus described is a prison. Could we not find schools to which it might equally well apply?

# 6

## *Religious and Moral Education*

FORMAL EDUCATION is rarely even the major element among the the forces which are affecting our pupils. They are exposed to the pressure of their total social environment, and the nature of that environment is particularly important in any consideration of religious and moral education. We cannot assume that children will have had any contact with religion in their lives away from school: we cannot even be sure that they will have been brought up to accept the traditional ideas of morality. Many parents, of course, pay lip service to religion. Some will send their children to Church or Sunday School while staying away themselves, and there is still a feeling that organised Christianity is respectable. The fact remains however that, in a school which is inside the state system, when a teacher faces a class he finds no universally accepted moral or religious ideas among its members. What must be strongly emphasised, because it is so often overlooked, is that precisely the same generalisation is true of the teaching staffs of schools, which may be expected to include atheists, agnostics, conventional believers, real believers and the group who are completely indifferent and fail to give religion even a moment's thought. In many staff rooms, those who teach Scripture are very conscious of their isolation from their colleagues.

Even a quick glance at the environment in which our pupils are growing up will remind us of the influences which surround them. The outside world is dominated by the forces of materialism. The economic system is based upon the profit motive, and what matters is will an article sell, not what is its value to society.

97

The pressure of advertisement, on every hoarding, on television, on every page of our newspapers and magazines, reminds us of the importance of this world's goods, and we find ourselves buying articles which we did not know we wanted. Conspicuous consumption has replaced the satisfaction of needs: we must keep up with the Joneses at all costs. The popular catch-phrases of yesterday—'you've never had it so good', and 'I'm all right, Jack!' offer an illuminating glimpse of our attitudes. If the economic system fails to offer us an adequate financial reward, we can always fall back upon bingo, football pools, greyhound- or horse-racing to provide us with the status symbols which we worship.

The second important feature of contemporary life is its emphasis upon entertainment: the right to be entertained must now be added to the list of the rights of man. The place of sport in the life of the nation amounts almost to a religion in itself: if we add television, cinema and radio, it sometimes looks as if the entire population has degenerated into one massive audience, a group of perpetual spectators.

Our young people are growing up then in this sort of world. In addition, as I have already pointed out, they are subjected to the pressures of their own teenage sub-culture. How can we expect boys and girls, who may be trying to live up to higher standards than many of their contemporaries, to stand up against the influences which surround them? How can they, wanting ardently to be grown-up, avoid taking their standards from the adults they see around them? Indeed, we get the teenagers we deserve, although to judge from the spate of lectures and articles which deplore the low moral standards of the young, one might not think so. It seems to me absurd to attempt a comparison between the standards of young people today and those at some time in the past: accurate evidence is missing, and those who wish to make odious comparisons rely usually on highly subjective impressions. In my own personal experience, I am alternately encouraged and discouraged by the adolescents I meet— a process which seems to have been continuing with very little change throughout a teaching career lasting more than thirty years.

How, indeed, can we bring up our children against this sort of background? The Christian Churches themselves retain their hold over only a minority of the people of the country, and make little appeal to the others. Many 'working-class' families have never been connected with a religious group, and regard religion as a middle-class interest which is not for them. Most Englishmen are frankly indifferent to religion, and allow it little influence over their lives. At the extreme, there is real hostility and contempt. Many regard Christianity as an outworn superstition, long since exploded by scientific discoveries: to them science and religion are in complete opposition. We are facing today the results of two generations of religious apathy and decline.

There are, however, two factors in the situation which are more encouraging. Most people still retain some lingering respect for Christian ideas of morality. We are living on our inherited moral capital, but there are few who lack some notion of what constitutes decent behaviour, which is derived however distantly from the Christian tradition. Those of us who teach in schools are well aware that, on the whole, parents expect schools to be more Christian in outlook than they are in their own homes. They want their children to live up to standards which are higher than their own, and they certainly expect their children's teachers to have very high standards. What an outcry there would be if teachers were to use certain Sunday newspapers in the classroom, even from parents who have no hesitation in taking these newspapers into their own homes.

The second helpful factor is that one of the results of higher education has been to produce a body of cultured and enlightened opinion which it is fashionable to call humanist. The humanist has a genuine interest in ethical problems, and recognises the need for moral, though not for religious, training. Such opinions have a great deal of influence on the intelligent sixth-former, especially if he is a scientist, when he is trying to work out his own values and principles. Although some orthodox Christian opinion will no doubt be shocked when I say so, I repeat that I regard this as an encouraging sign. It seems to me a matter of regret that many official Christians deplore the spread of humanism and even try to ignore it.

Before we can discuss the part which can be played by the school in religious and moral education, we must take a look at what is done by Church and Home. Church and chapel influence only a proportion of the young people of the country, many of whom are repelled by what seem to them traditional and conventional attitudes which are out of touch with life in the middle of the twentieth century. An authoritarian approach, a lack of imagination in handling adolescents, an undue concentration on theology, these seem almost calculated to put off the young person who may be genuinely seeking help and enlightenment. What a difference can be made by a stimulating personality who gives the impression that he lives in the real world and has a vital concern for those with whom he comes into contact! Is it not true to say that, in this case, it is the personality rather than the message which attracts? It seems to this writer that the Christian Churches need to do a great deal of thinking both about their approach to the young and about their doctrine.

The place where moral training occurs is, of course, the home. Much of this training occurs naturally and unconsciously. The standards which the parents themselves adopt have a vital effect on the children. If the parents tell lies to evade a difficult situation, they must not be surprised if their children do the same. If parents can see nothing wrong in pilfering or picking up an unguarded trifle, their children are likely to steal. If parents respect other human beings for what they find them to be worth, regardless of class, colour, sex or opinions, their children will probably behave in the same way. How far a person can give himself in affection to another human being may depend on the nature of his own home background. All this comes about, not by direct and conscious moral teaching, but through the example of someone who is loved by the child. Firm, not flexible and wavering standards are important. Criticism, discipline and punishment are needed on occasion, and are vitally necessary if the child is ever to learn self-control and self-discipline. Many parents are lazy, however, and find it difficult to trouble themselves unless their convenience is seriously attacked. Some have no clear standards of their own. Others are vaguely kind-hearted and want their children to be happier than they remember they were themselves; as a result they allow their children far too many liberties, and in particular perhaps give them too much pocket money. When a child says 'I want', it is of great importance for him to learn sometimes that he cannot have. Often parents treat their children in a way which amounts to real neglect, though sometimes—like the attitude of the Turks to their empire in the eighteenth century—it is neglect tempered by occasional massacre. Many children grow up without clear standards in the home, and in these cases parents experience particular difficulty at the time of adolescence, since it is far too late then to begin to insist on the observance of rules. Home can, then, lay the foundations of an effective training: unfortunately it often fails to do so.

When we come to examine the work of the school in religious and moral education, many considerations arise. First, it must be made clear that when I use the term education, I mean much more than a process of conditioning. Education is concerned with the making of persons, of individuals capable of self-determination. A mature man should be able to rise above his circumstances: he should be the captain of his soul. There can, therefore, be no imposition of beliefs or standards: throughout, we must preserve a scrupulous respect for the intellectual and spiritual freedom of our pupils. The acceptance of opinions, let alone beliefs, can have little value unless it is the free and responsible act of the individual. It is much more important to get pupils to think for themselves than to get them to think as we do. Religious education in school cannot be a matter of indoctrination, or a missionary activity concerned with the saving of souls.

Many people, including a number of clergymen, regard it as the main task of the school to make up for the deficiencies of the home and for the low standards of society. It is often said that religious education in the state school is a failure, and that the compromise which was embodied in the Education Act of 1944 is quite useless. In my view, this attitude to the task of the school is completely mistaken. I want to say, bluntly, that it cannot be the function of the schools to produce Christians, in the present climate of opinion, and that anyone who expects the schools to be able to send out a Christian generation has moved so far from reality that his opinions are hardly worth considering. How can a school effectively teach Christianity to a pupil who is pre-disposed by his upbringing and background to allow religion no place in his life? It is an important principle, when we are teaching children, that we should start from the place where they are—not from the place where we should like them to be: it is no easy task to confront a class of 15-year-olds who are all in different places, varying from the convinced Christian on the one hand to the aggressively agnostic young scientist on the other. Even if circumstances were more favourable, however, I should still feel that it is not the function of the schools to produce Christians, in the sense of members of the Christian Church. We may hope that our pupils will become interested in religion, and that some of them may be willing to give the Christian way of life a trial in their own lives: beyond that, I do not think we should be expected to go.

Speaking to the Annual Conference of the Head Mistresses' Association in June, 1962, Canon Lampe, Ely Professor of Divinity at Cambridge, stated that 'Religious teaching has to be biblical, doctrinal and ethical altogether, and divinity teaching demands specialist teachers who are committed Christians.' This conception is, of course, very different from my own. To begin with, the schools find it difficult to attract committed Christians who are willing and able to teach this most difficult of all subjects. Where a school simply cannot provide teachers of this sort, would the Professor prefer that religious education should cease? Even where such teachers are available, far too many of them fail to communicate effectively with their pupils. We do, indeed, need well-qualified teachers, but the qualifications must not be purely academic: some are able to be as authoritarian in this subject as the teacher of Mathematics in his. The good teacher must not be encased in an impregnable suit of doctrinal armour: he must be flexible both in mind and approach, and needs above all else to be able to perform the imaginative feat of putting himself in his pupil's place. Apart from all this, however, in my view the teacher in the maintained grammar school must have a more limited aim than that prescribed by the Professor of Divinity. I hope, below, to state clearly what I think that aim should be.

We often overlook the fact that there are very definite limits to what can be accomplished by direct exposition and exhortation in the sphere of religious and moral education, as is well known even to the most eloquent and skilful of preachers. I am profoundly convinced that religion is more likely to be caught than taught, and whether it is caught or not depends very much on the quality of the persons with whom the growing child is in contact. Any responsible adult—relative, parson, teacher of any subject, youth club leader, scoutmaster, probation officer—can provide the source of inspiration. He offers a pattern and a stimulus: from him the boy will take advice, comfort, criticism and, if necessary, even discipline. Admiration and hero-worship can be valuable if the grown-up concerned has high standards, and enough discernment to see what is taking place. A teacher of high calibre, who has the 'ear' of his pupils and can be seen by them as one who tries to express his principles in his own life, will achieve a valuable influence over them no matter what his academic qualifications in Divinity may be.

In any consideration of the possibility of religious education, the nature of the whole community is of great importance. The school should be based on trust and goodwill, not on fear and repression: in a word, it should be friendly. It should not be dominated by materialist values nor should there be too much emphasis on competition, either between person and person or group and group. The headmaster should not be attempting an impersonation of Jehovah: the staff should be sympathetic, understanding and permissive. In any staff room, two groups may be detected: those who, when asked if a pupil may do something slightly unusual, feel an automatic tendency to say 'no!' and those who would always say 'yes!'. In this sense, far more yes-men are needed. As a child grows older, he should be able to see the school as a moral community of which he is a full member, a community which itself has high standards and valuable traditions, and which can be seen to refuse to adopt low standards as a way out of a difficult situation. The schools must do far more to give pupils the opportunity to be of practical service to other people, refugees, old-age pensioners, handicapped children, those in need in any country of the world: the children should be encouraged to practise service in which they sacrifice their personal convenience for the benefit of other people. Practical experience which develops a sense of obligation is worth far more than theoretical knowledge that one ought to help. Adolescents cannot become responsible unless we give them some challenge to respond to. The school should be a co-operative community with a secure place in it for everyone, including those whose work is not very good and even those who are unsuccessful at games. All persons must be valued for their own sakes and never 'used' by others. Without this sort of atmosphere, the most brilliant Scripture teaching and the most eloquent head-magisterial homilies are in vain. There can be no attempt more barren than to give religious teaching in a school when it is obvious that the whole spirit of the school is opposed to that teaching.

Each school day normally begins with a religious service at which the whole school is present, and this should not be a mere opening ceremony but rather a preparation for the school day. The pupils should realise that it is their own service, not a dull formality imposed upon them by authority in obedience to the law of the land. The service should be based upon a simple theme, which suits the experience of the children and is within their range of interests. In this connection, the needs of the younger children should not be forgotten: it is a mistake to aim always at the sixth-former. Indeed, Junior Assemblies, apart from the rest of the school, may be helpful from time to time. As many members of the school as possible should take part, in planning the service, choosing the hymn or reading the lesson. Where possible a choir and orchestra should be used. The readings must be carefully chosen and very varied, from modern translations of the Bible and from sources outside the Bible. It is important to avoid a feeling of monotony: the average pupil has no use for vain repetitions.

Whatever is done, it is worth remembering that usually only a proportion of the gathering will be listening at any particular moment, and one can easily exaggerate the value of School Assembly for this reason. At times, however, one becomes aware that the attention of everyone present is concentrated on what is taking place, and it is worth going to considerable trouble to increase the number of such occasions, since they offer the opportunity to establish a real sense of community and to communicate much that is valuable. One of the most electrifying moments which I remember in School Assembly occurred when a member of the English staff began to read a passage from John Masefield's *The Everlasting Mercy*, in the local accent. Every boy was listening hard, and it became clear, as the week progressed, that the boys were looking forward each morning to the next instalment. Is this to be described as an undignified experiment? If our assemblies are dull—and they often are—whose fault is it? Put at its lowest, however, the School Assembly is a daily reminder that religion exists and that some people have a place for it in their lives: we have to remember that, for many, this may be the only reminder.

The content of the Scripture (Divinity or Religious Knowledge) period is normally laid down by an 'Agreed Syllabus', agreed that is by a conference consisting of representatives of the Churches, teachers and local education authorities. I find these syllabuses a valuable guide and a useful technical help, but I do not regard myself as bound by them: as a general principle, I should refuse to be dictated to by any outside authority as to what I should teach, in these or any other lessons.

In my opinion, the first three years of the course should be used to give necessary information to a child growing up in what is still, nominally, a Christian country. They should be taught the story of the life of Jesus, and made familiar with the famous stories from the Old and New Testaments. They should hear of the activities of great Christians throughout the ages and in contemporary life. It is important that children should not be given the impression that Christianity is something which happened in the past, and it may be a real help to some of them to learn about Christian principles being applied in modern conditions. In addition, of course, an attempt must be made at a simple explanation of what Christianity is about and what a Christian believes. If the teacher is himself a committed Christian, he ought to be able to communicate sincerely what this means to him.

Between the ages of 14 and 16, when the pupil has become interested in himself in relation to other people, the direct exposition of what is meant by Christianity should recede into the background. The centre of interest becomes the child's own problems and difficulties, though Christian standards should be made plain of course. The object is to help the pupil to make up his own mind about his own behaviour, motives and attitudes. All the time there is need for frank discussions, which must seem relevant to the members of the group, dealing with their relations with their parents, their friends, the other sex and the adult world in general. I feel that, by the time he has reached 16, a boy should have been made aware of his need to acquire his own values, and that he should be conscious of the low standards which exist in the outside world in which he will have to live and work—this seems to me an essential preparation for the school leaver. By this time, he ought to be giving some thought to his duty to his neighbour: his attention should be directed to the need for self-control and self-discipline, particularly if he is inclined to resent control from an outside authority. He will need constant reminders about the unique value of each human personality. Where possible, he should be thinking of his duty to God. If the school can accomplish as much as this, it will have done marvels. More often, it will achieve only a partial success, but it has to be remembered that many pupils will leave school at 16, and that this may well be their last contact with discussions of this sort.

The sixth form offers a unique opportunity in the school system to help the adolescent to hammer out his own principles. In my experience, such a person resents dogmatism and any attempt to impose ideas and attitudes. A strong element feels that religion has outlived its usefulness and has no relevance to life as it is lived in 1965. I have often been asked a question like the following: 'How can you, presumably an intelligent man, believe in the existence of God?'

When faced with this fundamental question, I accept the implied compliment as gracefully as possible and try to answer it honestly. There follows a series of far-ranging discussions which lasts for many weeks. In answering, I make no attempt to convert anyone to my point of view, but try to show that a presumably intelligent man can believe in the existence of God in 1965, that there is no essential conflict between the scientist and the religious man, that to be an atheist is at least as 'unintelligent' as to be a theist and that the agnostic position, while useful perhaps as a temporary resting-place, must obviously leave many questions unanswered and many problems unsolved. I hope that, in discussions of this sort, Christian, agnostic, atheist and the boy who is quite indifferent may at least gain in mutual understanding. It must be clear that, at this stage, the Synoptic problem and the Gospel according to St. John are irrelevant, and any attempt to expound Christian doctrine would be a waste of time. I find it impossible to regard this as an opportunity to produce convinced Christians, even if I thought it my function to attempt to do so. I am happy if I send out into the world boys who have a vital interest in the matters I have been discussing, and who are well on the way towards sorting out their own position. Some of them may well wish to attach themselves to a Christian Church, but that is their business, not mine. I will tell them what I believe and why I believe it when they ask, and they usually do.

Apart from all this, the sixth-former is anxious to discuss a whole host of subjects, and discuss is the operative word. Some of them wish to hear details of the faiths of the different Christian denominations. Others are interested in comparative religion and demand to be told about the other great religions of the world. Many pupils insist upon a really detailed examination of the question 'can a scientist be a religious man?' Even those who have little interest in religion are prepared to discuss problems of morals and ethics. The politicians are keen to think about morality and the Bomb, pacifism, the ethics of the capitalist system, of advertising, of capital punishment. Others prefer to deal with personal morality and their relations with other people. A whole range of topics centering on sex and marriage inevitably come up for discussion. Qualities like courage, honesty, charity, sincerity, provoke much earnest thought and produce some surprising conclusions. From time to time, the Religion and Philosophy series of broadcasts of the BBC may be used: it has to be said, however, that only a minority of these are successful in striking the level which the boys appreciate.

Many people appear to think that the Scripture lesson is the only period in the timetable which is concerned with religious and moral education: this is, of course, a serious error. Obviously the teacher's own approach to his subject, whatever it may be, can make a tremendous difference to the impression which is made upon the pupils. In particular, whether he starts with materialist or spiritual assumptions will affect the whole colour of his teaching. An education which is deep enough to nourish the imagination, and a training in the recognition of valuable experiences, can be obtained through many subjects. Mathematics and Science are often taught from a completely rationalist angle, but it is possible to convey the idea that emotional and aesthetic judgments are important and ethical considerations · very real. A scientist who is a Christian will make it clear that qualitative as well as quantitative factors are important, and that Science and Religion are complementary not in opposition: and it is particularly valuable that impressions like these should come from such a source.

Subjects like Literature and the Humanities compel us to face facts about human nature and the human spirit, and enlarge the range of our experience. The arts show how a creative civilised person has selected events in his own life or experience and has found meaning and coherence in them. The artist helps to quicken the human spirit to a greater degree of awareness. From a subject like History we can learn a better insight into human motives and a deeper understanding of human character. Colour prejudice, a lack of understanding of foreigners, parents or the rich are all due, surely, to a lack of imagination. The imagination must be called to life and stimulated by something richer than comics, science fiction and the majority of television programmes. There is a need for the acquisition of critical standards, for intellectual integrity based on critical judgment, for the ability to see both sides of the case and to understand that men have mixed motives. In how many quarrels, in history or in our own personal lives, shall we find one side arrayed completely in white and the other in black? It is valuable to learn to distinguish between the varying shades of grey. In these numerous ways, the different subjects of the curriculum can do a great deal of the work which is preliminary to moral and religious education.

If I turn aside to consider the special problem of sexual morality, I do so, not because I am so misguided as to think that morality is identical with sexual morality, but because of the particular difficulty which this problem presents today. Boys and girls grow up among many influences which are sexually stimulating and many temptations to sexual laxity. Their own problem can be summed up in the typical teenage question 'Why shouldn't we?' There is a clear need for guidance which ideally, of course, should come from the home, but in the great majority of cases parents fail their children in this respect, and the school has to step in. During the first year in the school the biological facts of sex should be taught in the ordinary science lesson, before the child becomes emotionally involved: accurate information is essential, and if the lessons serve no other purpose they will at least enable children to call things by their proper names. Between the ages of 14 and 16, in the Scripture lesson, the chance should be taken to discuss the Christian attitude towards sex and marriage, together with the personal problems of the pupils. This should be done by a teacher with whom the children can talk freely and who has high standards. Only a proportion of the pupils can be expected to join in the actual discussion, but often those who say least benefit most from what takes place. As I have indicated above, the sixth form gives an excellent opportunity for a full examination of the whole question. At this stage, the discussions are often amazingly frank, and there can be little doubt of their value to the sixth-formers themselves.

Relations with the other sex should not be regarded as something special which must be discussed in isolation, and certainly not with an outside speaker: this topic should be regarded as part of a continuing discussion which covers the whole range of personal relationships. The underlying principle throughout must surely be that of the unique value of each human personality, which can be stated either as part of the Christian position or as a self-evident proposition, depending on circumstances. In matters of sex, the danger must be avoided of giving the impression of a completely negative attitude, of a concentration on a list of things which must not be done. A respect for the integrity of other people must obviously demand some self-denial from us, but this needs to be put positively. The answer to the blunt question, why postpone sexual gratification to some future time when you can enjoy it now, must be to emphasise that the value of deliberate self-control lies in providing the best possible conditions for a happy marriage. If there follows the question what is so marvellous about marriage, a question which comes usually out of an unhappy experience, an attempt has to be made to describe a relationship which grows and develops, and gives two human beings the environment in which they can become complete persons. If you cannot face difficult questions like these, and above all if you are shocked by them, you have no business to engage in this sort of teaching. Throughout it is important to get across the point, vividly illustrated, that each person must expect to be faced quite frequently by difficult choices between different lines of action. A moral action implies choice by an individual, thinking and deciding for himself. The school must help him to become aware of the need to make this sort of decision, and must start him off on the difficult task of working out values and standards for himself.

Those who stand in the place of parents have a particularly hard task when they engage in this aspect of education. Their attentions are unwelcome to some of the pupils. What they are trying to do contrasts violently with the attitudes of most adults outside the school, and yet the outside world appears to have the most astonishingly naïve expectations of what the school is able to accomplish. For example, it is ludicrous to expect the schools to prevent juvenile delinquency, or to give children immunity from the greed, the cynicism and the sexual pressures so obvious in the outside world. Against all this, the school can set only the influence of a few upright men (who in the eyes of the adolescent have not notably achieved success in life, in an age when success can be held to justify almost anything), a limited amount of time in the classroom and in Assembly, and at best the inspiring fact of belonging to a moral community. The sort of education I have described is slow to take effect and, indeed, often appears to have none. It is cumulative in its influence and its results may not be visible for many years. The teachers concerned have to rely on the unconscious effects on the young which their own standards may be having. It is their task to try to be the sort of person they want their boys and girls to become, and at the same time to be the sort of person they will come to for help and advice. A mistake to be avoided is to pitch your standards so high that ordinary mortals cannot live up to them, and give up trying in discouragement.

The Scripture teacher has to avoid two contradictory mistakes: on the one hand there is the danger which arises from making dogmatic authoritarian pronouncements on what is right and wrong, on what action should be taken. This approach is likely to arouse maximum opposition, and even to have the contrary effect to the one which is intended. On the other hand, there is the danger of permissive attitudes which give no guidance at all, and which lead to a discussion of different points of view while leaving the individual substantially unaided. Not everyone is capable of thinking things out entirely alone, and many children (and adults) find it so easy to accept the least demanding solution. If we leave our adolescents without interference to fend for themselves, may this not drive them to accept their pop cuture uncritically and swallow their teenage conventions whole? What is needed is a genuine discussion, a meeting of minds when superficial opinions are exposed and prejudices attacked, and the pupils are gradually brought to think deeply and clearly about the fundamental questions which they love to raise.

I am by no means defeatist about the opportunities which face the school, but I do not think that direct religious education is often possible. We are more likely to be engaged in what Professor Jeffreys, in his book *Beyond Neutrality*, has called prereligious education, in removing the obstacles, in preparing the way. In doing this, we obviously need the help of far more, and better, teachers in all subjects, men and women who are prepared to resist the standards of the world, and who will try to live up to the tremendous demands which will be made on them. It has to be admitted that many Scripture lessons are an almost complete failure, because they are so academic and remote from real life, and that there are many schools which fail to produce the atmosphere in which religious education can even be attempted.

The situation must also be faced that a direct connection with one of the Christian churches exists in the lives of only a minority of the inhabitants of this country. Under these circumstances, much of what passes for Christian education in the maintained school is superficial and unreal, partly because of the inadequacies of the teachers themselves, but mainly as a result of the situation in the world outside. Unless the aim of religious teaching in schools is thought to be indoctrination or a process of conditioning, and if it is I for one shall object and refuse to have any part in it, would it not be better to stop the pretence and concentrate on what is both possible and useful? Most Agreed Syllabuses lose contact with reality when the pupil reaches the age of 14, if they have not already done so. Before that, he should learn about the life of Jesus, about Christian beliefs and attitudes, about the way in which many men and women have attempted to express these in their lives and are still attempting to do so. Before or after 14, I can see no point in geographical explorations of the Eastern Mediterranean or an introduction to the intricacies of the 1st and 2nd Isaiah—better to explore the needs and difficulties of the pupils themselves and direct their attention to the complex task of constructing a personal philosophy of life among the conflicting ideas, attitudes and pressures which are to be found in modern society. No child should be allowed to grow up ignorant of the Christian foundations of our modern civilisation, but he must be given a realistic basis for life as he will find it in the world outside the school. In a sense it is true to say that the inflated aims, and claims, of Scripture syllabuses are a major obstacle in the way of their achieving even a meagre degree of success. Nothing short of a revolutionary change in our approach can help the schools to pass on this part of our cultural heritage. When Jesus said 'I am come that they might have life and that they might have it more abundantly', he was surely expressing what should be the aim of all who are engaged in the work of education.

# 7

# *Out of School*

IT IS a long-established tradition that a well-conducted school
will provide out of school activities in which the pupils can spend
at least part of their leisure time. These are essentially voluntary
in that the pupil decides for himself if he will join in any of
them, and if he does he chooses the ones which interest him.
Since these clubs and societies offer, among other things, a
valuable complement to what goes on inside the classroom and
may well help to meet a particular need of a pupil, it is legitimate
to propel him gently in the appropriate direction. A quiet, reserved boy or girl may benefit greatly from membership of a
debating or discussion society and will often grow quickly both
in confidence and articulateness. A brash, loud-mouthed young
man may be helped to discipline his own speech by taking up
acting seriously, and may well learn to control his own feelings
by giving tongue to the turbulent outbursts of others. The school
must not, however, take offence if a senior pupil rejects the
opportunities which it provides, and prefers his own activities
apart from the school. A friendly conversation on the subject
may reveal important reasons why this is happening (such as
an inability to mix with other pupils, a strong sexual attraction
or an acute shortage of money which makes a part-time job
urgently necessary), and it may be possible to give help or advice.
But in the last resort the pupil must be free to choose—these are
voluntary out of school activities.

In the case of the first-generation grammar school child there
is often a particular need for chosen activities of this kind. If he
is interested in music, the boy may select the jazz club, the jazz

band, the pop group, the orchestra, the choir or he may prefer
to join those who listen to classical music. If his interests lie in
a more literary direction, he may choose to spend his leisure time
in the literary society, the writers' club, the poetry club or the
dramatic society. An art society offers different opportunities for
self expression and the development of a number of individual
tastes. The point here is that these societies help a boy to follow
up an interest which he already has or to develop one which is
quite new. They supplement what the school is trying to do in
other ways and do it all the more convincingly because the pupil
has chosen for himself, and is not the unwilling recipient of the
cultural propaganda of his teachers. It is likely, too, that timetable exigencies have deprived some pupils of the chance to carry
further an interest in music or the visual arts, and under these
circumstances the club has an even greater value.

Some schools have adopted the practice of starting clubs and
societies inside normal school time while expecting them to continue in the pupils' own time afterwards. This may be forced
on a school which serves a wide area and is afflicted by a rigid
bus timetable, and is a method of ensuring that all pupils spend
at least some time in at least one activity. On the other hand, it
may have the result of confining societies to a particular afternoon, and may give the impression that they are under the
control of the staff. Genuinely voluntary societies should be
managed by the senior pupils who gain valuable experience in
taking responsibility and in learning the arts of organisation.
Mistakes will certainly be made and may be pointed out gently
by the member of staff who exercises a distant supervision: they
will, no doubt, be pointed out much more forcibly by members
of the group concerned. In any case, do we not learn by our own
mistakes and sometimes even by the errors of others?

As more schools devote a considerable part of their timetable
to general studies, particularly in the sixth form but also spreading down into the fourths and fifths, it may be that they will
wish to integrate certain of their out-of-school activities with the
cultural period inside the timetable. One can easily see fifth
formers, for example, enjoying unexamined work which they
have chosen to do and deciding to let this overflow outside school
hours, and granted some flexibility and imagination in timetable
making this should easily be possible. After all, if you have

reached a critical point in painting a picture, or if you are enjoying a recording of Tschaikowsky's 5th Symphony, you do not want to stop when the bell goes. This principle already operates with regard to games and most pupils are happy to continue after school.

Today, most schools are willing to offer their pupils a wide choice of physical activities outside school, even if compulsory games inside the timetable remain very limited in number. There are still schools which regard with a peculiar sanctity the games which they have (arbitrarily) decided to adopt as if, in some areas, Rugby football were demonstrably superior to Association, whereas in others, by some strange chance, the reverse were true. In such cases it is usually true that masters will keep a tight control of games and the selection of teams—school games are too important to be entrusted to pupils! The serious problem arises, however, when pupils are expected to represent the school in their own free time, for example on Saturday afternoon. If a boy much prefers to play soccer for his club to the honour of representing his school at rugger, whole acres of barren controversy may be opened up, with much discussion of what constitutes loyalty to the school, much taking of offence on both sides and much loss of a sense of proportion. Is it not clear, however, that a boy should be free to spend his Saturday afternoons as he likes and that he will only play with conviction and success a game which he enjoys? In other words, membership of school teams should represent a voluntary decision on the part of the pupil. Even if the school teams are weakened by the defection of brilliant, but unwilling, players has the end of the world arrived? In any case, I cannot see why a sixth-former should be subjected to compulsory games, especially if he is not offered a considerable choice, and we have to remember that cricket is still hedged with a strange divinity. If he enjoys cross-country running, why should he not run: if he likes swimming and there is a bath available, why not? Badminton, Basket Ball, Hockey, Athletics are reputable winter sports, as are Tennis, Rowing and Athletics in summer, and why should they not be provided? To press the matter farther, if a school provides adequate physical education in its timetable, I can see little virtue in compelling a pupil of 18 to participate unwillingly in physical activities which he thinks, however mistakenly and arrogantly, are a waste of time or even ludicrous. Some people can see no sense in chasing balls or team games, and we have surely progressed beyond the day when we worshipped team spirit, undefined and unqualified.

A school should, then, offer many different kinds of physical activities and should encourage its senior pupils to find at least one among them which gives pleasure and satisfaction. For many boys and quite a number of girls a tremendous happiness is to be obtained by controlling and using the body effectively, and for them this is the most easily acquired and valuable form of self-expression. Time to be spent on training, on the achievement of muscular co-ordination, on weight-training and body-building, is given up willingly, almost in the spirit of devotion. Experience of success and the ability to excel in something are extremely important for the adolescent, and are most easily achieved by many of them in the physical sphere. Some express themselves most successfully in an agility or a gymnastic club: others prefer judo, some enjoy boxing, (and there is no reason why they should be deprived of this if there is careful supervision and control, and if there is neither compulsion to take part nor over per-suasion). Many girls obtain a great satisfaction from bodily movement to music. Both sexes enjoy walking, climbing, camp-ing, cycling, swimming, rowing or canoeing, either working through the Youth Hostels Association or the Duke of Edin-burgh's award, or with small groups of friends. The new sport of orienteering, on Scandinavian lines, offers exciting opportunities to many young people who dislike the more formal sports. The Outward Bound movement has captured the imagination of many. One sees, then, a school providing a vast array of oppor-tunities, especially for its senior pupils, and encouraging each individual to find at least one which he can enjoy as a matter of voluntary choice. There ought not to be a situation in which an entire senior school is playing cricket on the same afternoon—with perhaps forty-four boys genuinely enjoying themselves, while the rest (compulsorily) participate in what seems to them a dull, pointless and time-consuming operation.

In many schools it has become the practice to organise holiday parties whether inside this country or abroad, for many different purposes, cultural, linguistic or physical. This is an entirely laud-able endeavour which demands a great deal from the teachers who are in charge, and only some individuals have the patience, understanding and stamina which is needed. The real object of the visit should be clearly decided and made well-known: is it purely holiday or is it to be a working-party, and if the latter, exactly what will be expected of its members? Is the aim to find out as much as much as possible of the cultural life and ancient monuments of another country? Is it to be a climbing and mountaineering holiday? Is it to be a holiday visit with no other objective in mind than a vague feeling that it might do some general educational good? (and these are usually the least satisfactory). Party visits abroad are rarely useful from the point of view of learning languages, unless on arrival the party separates and individuals stay in ordinary homes. There are problems which arise out of different social customs in different countries, and it is as well, before starting, to find out what parents wish about smoking and the consumption of alcohol. Too wide an age-range is usually a mistake, since what may be permissible for 18-year-olds may be improper for children of 14—certainly in the eyes of their parents who are, after all, handing over their children to the care of the school in good faith. Only very experienced people should take children walking in mountainous country, and preferably the experience should be of the same mountains. Children should be properly equipped for heavy walking, and care should be taken not to expect too much from, for example, a town child who has never climbed a mountain in his life. As a result of the school's efforts, some of these may become addicts —others may find it much too much like hard work and long for the lights and the fish-and-chip shops of the city centre. Countless young people have been given a taste for holidays, by such parties, which are very different from those which may be experienced at Blackpool, Skegness or Southend.

There is no need here for a long discussion of the different uniformed organisations, though many schools participate in their activities. Scouts, Guides and the Boys Brigade are well known for the opportunities which they bring to their members: they have introduced a salutary but pleasant and unobtrusive discipline into the lives of boys and girls who, without them, might have found it hard to escape from the restrictions of town life and might have missed the chance to enjoy nature, the pleasures of camping and the satisfaction of learning how to look after themselves and others. When we discuss cadet forces we enter a much more controversial field. There can be no doubt that many schools, especially those of a socially pretentious character, have what is to all intents and purposes a compulsory cadet force, no matter how skilfully the pressure may be administered: why otherwise should so many schools set apart a section of the school day, said usually to be heavily over-subscribed, for this particular activity? Undoubtedly some boys thrive on the corps, and it is often felt that it should be provided for them if their numbers are great enough. No boy should be compelled to participate, and if he fails to do so should not be robbed of all chance of becoming a prefect. Many individuals find its 'yours not to reason why' type of discipline extremely irksome, and should not for that reason be subjected to it. It is easy to see why, in their book *Education and the Working Class*, Jackson and Marsden selected the corps as a particularly oppressive feature of school life, and the first-generation grammar school boy in particular is unlikely to respond to its general atmosphere. Indeed, its whole ethos appears to be contrary to the attitudes expressed elsewhere in this book on the matter of discipline, freedom and the proper development of the human personality. I must, therefore, express grave doubts as to its educational value and the propriety of its presence in an educational establishment.

To provide opportunities for self expression is an obvious aim of some of the societies which a school will provide. I have already mentioned musical activities of various kinds, and those concerned with literature, writing and acting. Among the latter should be found not only a school dramatic society aiming to produce a school play for the benefit of the whole school and its friends. One of the most vigorous activities at High Pavement School took the form of a House Dramatic Competition. For this purpose, each house prepared a short play (very often a series of extracts from a larger one) lasting about half an hour: it was produced, acted and stage-managed entirely by the boys themselves, and each year we were surprised by the high standard which was reached by many of these productions. Since there were eight houses, something like 150 boys were occupied in one capacity or another, and it was gratifying to notice how few of the houses bothered themselves with the hackneyed one-act plays so beloved of amateur dramatic societies.

## Out of School

A school debating society has an obvious place in helping pupils to develop their powers of self expression, especially if those who control it do not insist upon a strictly formal procedure. Many an inarticulate pupil has learned to speak reasonably in its comparatively sympathetic atmosphere, and has been grateful later for the impulse which took him to his first meeting. Others have learned to thrive in the completely informal atmosphere of a discussion society, where one broadens one's interests and opens one's mind, and at the same time becomes able to speak one's thoughts. Some discussion societies concentrate on current affairs, international and domestic, and bodies like the Council for Education in World Citizenship organise conferences and discussions on subjects in the international sphere. During the 1964 General Election schools in many parts of the country celebrated the occasion by holding their own Mock Election. A mock election can arouse a tremendous amount of interest and excitement: it provides an opportunity for a valuable education in democratic procedures, and the amount of nonsense which is spoken and blazoned forth on posters is not obviously greater than that which appears in the real thing.

A School Magazine may be a dull, formal affair which confines itself to a series of reports of what has become past history (and such reports have a definite value), or it may prefer to encourage the literary talents of the pupils. If it does the latter, the problem of censorship is likely to arise, sooner or later, and it may well affect the activities of the debating, discussion and dramatic societies as well. An official magazine which goes out from the school to governors, Education Committee and parents may well cause offence if it has encouraged complete freedom of speech, though one has met satire which was subtle enough to pass unremarked even by the most vigilant and conventional authorities. Some risks are well worth taking, but it is perhaps wiser to have another literary magazine which is produced by the pupils and circulates inside the school only. It is unfortunate that so many adults possess such a thin skin. Freedom of speech in debates and discussions is most important: there should be no attempt to bar political or religious subjects, and the staff must not be afraid of controversy which is the breath of life of societies like these: adults with tender susceptibilities should stay away. The discussion is a matter for the pupils: they will usually take the advice of a congenial member of staff, especially if it is given as advice and not as a royal command.

In many parts of the country there is no accessible bookshop, and even where one is available many grammar school children come from homes where no one would think of buying a book. A number of schools have therefore decided that it is their duty to take a great deal of trouble to encourage children to buy and possess books of their own. The tremendous number and range of paperbacks which now exist has made it possible for schools to open paperback bookshops at which pupils can buy not only books of specialist interest but others of a much more general nature. The opportunity to pick up books and browse in them is something which adolescents appreciate, and the step towards the foundation of a private library can easily be taken at small expense. Boys and girls who have lost the habit of visiting the public library, and who find the array of specialist books in the school library rather forbidding, will often buy paperbacks. Incidentally, the question arises why not provide a main school library, concerned mainly with non-specialist books and quite separate from the sixth form library? Most schools, in any case, have far too few books in their libraries and lack the services of a full-time librarian who could do a great deal to help and stimulate reading.

Many single-sex schools have decided that they have an obligation to provide for the social education of their senior pupils, and joint sixth form societies have been established between twin boys' and girls' schools. This official recognition of the fact that adolescent boys and girls are interested in each other has come as something of a shock to older members of staff of both sexes. Such a society can do a great deal to mitigate the narrowness of a monastic type of education, and can help young people to learn to understand and mix sensibly with each other in a planned series of activities which will often include ballroom dancing (a real boon to the clumsy, untrained male).

Without attempting a complete list of school clubs one must mention those which are an extension of the work done in academic subjects inside the classroom. Obviously, a boy who is fascinated by science will jump at the chance to broaden his interests in a scientific society, and the same is true of history, geography, languages, economics and mathematics. The hobbies which the pupils have themselves taken up may lead to the formation of still more clubs, concerned with photography, stamp collecting, handicrafts, engineering or chess (sometimes equipped with school teams, and even school colours). In some schools religious societies are to be found, whether a brand of the Student Christian Movement (which, like the C.E.W.C., organises valuable sixth form conferences), a religious discussion society or something much narrower in range and much less attractive.

Part of the duty of a good school is surely to direct the attention, particularly of its sixth-formers, towards the interesting opportunities for self development, which exist in the outside world. These will include important lectures and discussions, meetings of scientific, historical and other societies, and art exhibitions. The school will organise visits to these and to important concerts, to the local theatre if there is one and to valuable films. Sixth-formers should learn to join in the cultural activities of the neighbourhood while they are still at school, and if the school does not guide them in this direction some are unlikely to receive help from any other source.

One last type of out of school activity remains to be discussed —those concerned with service to people in need in the outside world. The idealism of the young leads many of them to feel that they want to help in some way, and it is legitimate for a school to encourage this feeling, to draw attention to ways in which it might be done and to help senior pupils to organise something positive. Some schools have organised an Old Peoples' Visiting Society which brings pupils in touch with old people who can be helped in a variety of ways—doing shopping, redecorating a room, gardening or even just regular social contacts which can be very comforting to those who are lonely. Other schools have interested individual pupils in the possibility of helping the unfortunate in other ways: these include part-time work as an orderly in a hospital, in a children's home, in a remand home, in a tough youth club in a slum area or with handicapped children. The development of a social conscience, the recognition that there is still much suffering in spite of an affluent society, and that all of us in one way or another share a responsibility for this is part of the equipment of a good citizen, and how better could a school be engaged than in stimulating its growth? This could lead on to a desire to take part in Voluntary Service Overseas or to spend part of one's working career in a backward country abroad.

Most schools, at some time or another, organise collections for deserving causes and much hard work and imagination have been successfully mobilised. Hardly a school in the country failed to contribute to the World Refugee Fund, and the World Hunger Campaign, Oxfam, and other similar causes have aroused great activity. Some schools have preferred to concentrate on local or national charities. Again, it would be thought that the outside world could only applaud these efforts of the young, especially as public opinion seems very ready to condemn them, on the slightest provocation. In some areas, however, one has seen the Education Committee limit collections and activities of this kind, on the ground that excessive pressure is brought on children to persuade them to give, and that some children (or their parents) are able to give more than others. It is at once pitiful and fascinating to observe the effects of timidity and a strictly limited view of the meaning of education on those who, in a few places, are lamentably responsible for the working of the education system.

Few would deny the benefit which may be obtained from clubs and societies, undertaken voluntarily, in broadening the interests, stimulating the activities and developing a sense of responsibilty in adolescents. The more limited the home background, the more valuable do these become. Is there not a place, however, for some greater integration with what is going on in society outside the school, and need the schools be so narrowly exclusive in their attempts to control the ways in which their pupils fill their private lives? After all, they have no monopoly rights over the leisure time of their pupils. If a school found it possible to work positively with a well-managed youth club, to share activities and even premises, might not both parties benefit? Among the courses which are organised by a lively College of Further Education there must be some which would be of great interest and value to senior pupils in a grammar school. The area which we have been discussing in this chapter is surely one in which it should be possible for a grammar school to enter positively into the life of its neighbourhood. It is unfortunate that some of them give the impression that, far from wishing to do this, they prefer to withdraw even farther from the life which goes on around them, and even worse sometimes imply that there is an acute danger of contamination. Need it be pointed out that those who suffer most in this assumed conflict of attitudes are those of their pupils who are very much part of the 'inferior' background, and who have to work out these very tensions in their own lives. Would it not be preferable for the grammar school to be a power-house of light and culture throughout its district and to recognise that it has some obligations to the greater society, as well as to its individual members?

# 8

# *Leaving School*

ONE READS, repeatedly, complaints that many pupils receive little guidance about their careers and that others are wrongly advised because of the lack of information and skill of those who guide them. It is natural that the teachers who have watched over the progress of a pupil for many years, and who have gradually learned to understand him, should be concerned to see that he embarks upon a career which is suitable and which will give him a chance to use his abilities for the good of society. Obviously many teachers possess neither the personal qualities nor the time and knowledge which would make them effective career advisers. Most schools, therefore, appoint a particular member of staff to give guidance about careers and he and the head of the school usually do most of this work between them. Since it is impossible for the careers master or mistress to be spared from teaching, much of the work has to be done in out of school time and free periods, and if it is possible the teacher concerned may be allowed more free periods than his colleagues. The head of the school frequently deals with the 18-year-old leavers, and therefore has on his hands the whole complicated problem of advice about University entry though, if he is sensible, he will see that much preliminary work is done by others. There may well be therefore, in a particular school, a situation in which the work is shared by two people who have neither the time nor the qualifications which would enable them to do it properly, and there are many who feel that this way of managing careers guidance shows the English love of amateurism at its most dangerous.

## Leaving School

In each local government area, there exists a Youth Employment Office, sometimes as a part of the education service, sometimes as a section of the local office of the Ministry of Labour. Here, at least in theory, is a group of experts who are thoroughly trained in vocational guidance and have all the necessary knowledge of careers, both local and national, at their finger-tips. The Report of the Ince Committee (1945) recommended that the Youth Employment Service should take over the whole work of vocational guidance and should rely on the schools to provide the detailed information about their clients when they come for advice. This was intended to cover all school leavers at all ages, and if it operated effectively it would certainly relieve the school of a vast amount of time-consuming work which, in many cases, not many of them are equipped to do properly.

Unfortunately, the realities of the position today are far different. Although there are many devoted, well-equipped and properly qualified officers in the Youth Employment Service, it is still a fact that fewer than half have received an adequate training. In most areas the service is badly understaffed, and would be quite unable to take over the complete burden of career work from all the schools. Some of the work done is perfunctory, and gives the impression to the outsider of a desire rather to fill vacancies than to place boys and girls in a career to which they are suited. A fifteen minute interview, and this is the standard practice in many parts of the country, is quite inadequate for the purpose in many cases. The Youth Employment Service suffers from two important shortages, a lack of adequately trained officers and a great shortage of numbers. To begin with, there is an obvious need for the career of Youth Employment Officer to be developed into a major social service with salaries and conditions of work which would make it really attractive to the able men and women who could find in its ranks a worthwhile and fascinating career.

Under these circumstances, it is not surprising that many grammar schools prefer to play an active part in career work, with greater or lesser co-operation with the Youth Employment Office. There are Youth Employment Officers who regard this as a piece of typical grammar school exclusiveness, perhaps with justice in some cases. It seems inevitable however, that, until the service is built up both in numbers and quality to enable it to cope effectively with the rapidly growing problem, schools must continue to concern themselves with the careers of their leavers. A compromise is often adopted which makes the school work closely with youth employment officers over pupils who leave at 16, while keeping in their own hands the guidance of sixth-formers. What is clear, of course, is a need for the closest possible co-operation of school and office for the benefit of the pupils concerned: this involves a degree of personal understanding between careers master and employment officer which is not always achieved. It is unfortunate that, in this important field, an attitude almost of armed neutrality has come into existence, with a feeling on the one hand of intrusion in the affairs of a school and a suspicion on the other hand of an amateurish and ineffective guidance.

In the school which I know best, we were fortunate in having the happiest relations with a lively and thoroughly efficient Youth Employment Office which was helpful and co-operative in every conceivable way. We tried hard to arouse an interest in careers during a boy's fourth year in the school by both general discussions in house groups and personal interviews with the careers master. At this stage many boys had already decided that they would stay in the sixth form. Those who had not made this decision met, during their fifth year, the careers master and Youth Employment Officer together, at school. Parents had, during these years, several opportunities to discuss these matters with house master, headmaster or careers master. The Parent Staff Association made a practice of organising a meeting each year which was devoted to a detailed discussion of some particular careers, and from time to time the Youth Employment Office organised for the school (and for many visiting schools) a Careers Convention or an Exhibition. This event did something to excite interest and to dramatise the situation. There are always, of course, a number of parents who prefer to make their own arrangements for the careers of their sons: here the school can do little but attempt to prevent a bad mistake from being made. It is important to emphasise that, in the last resort, the school and even the Youth Employment Service can only give advice. They are in no position to direct juveniles into particular occupations, even if the nation has a great need for vacancies to be filled, and it would be improper for them to try to do so.

Naturally, they will draw attention to the special needs of the community, but their first pre-occupation must be to start off the school leaver in a career which is best for him.

As far as sixth form careers were concerned, the school kept the initiative in its own hand, though whenever there was a need for further information about a particular career a sixth-former would be advised to visit the Youth Employment Office. On top of all its other work, the Employment Service could not possibly have undertaken the guidance of 170 sixth-formers. Quite apart from this, it seems impossible to discuss a sixth-former's future with him, in any effective way, without a personal knowledge of the boy and his background which cannot be transferred to any form which has yet been devised. In the case of the sixth-former, career guidance and personal advice tend to become so closely interwoven that it is difficult to see how an outside person can do much more than give factual information which is, or can easily be made, accessible in another form. Inside the school one found that a discussion with an individual boy, which began with a request for guidance about a career or a University application, would range over his interests and activities, his home circumstances, the degree of his application to his work, his love affairs, the level of his academic attainment and even the style of his haircut. In these circumstances surely, personal knowledge and a reasonably close human relationship are worth much more than a great deal of technical knowledge. If there were available a vocational guidance officer who had at his finger tips information about all the careers which are relevant to a particular boy's subjects and interests and who at the same time was particularly skilled at working with boys of 17 and 18, we can see that an interview with him would be valuable if only because an outside view would be brought to bear. Even this could not take the place of the continuous discussions which happen at any time, during a boy's sixth form career. Among other things, how could the vocational guidance expert find the time or the opportunity for this kind of discussion? If the school cannot manage without outside help—and at the moment its teaching staff lack the time and expertise to do so—advice and guidance for the sixth-former must be a co-operative enterprise of two people, one who has expert knowledge of the opportunities which exist and one who knows well, and has frequent access to, the individual boy or girl. If this is true of the sixth former, it seems likely, too, that it will be true of the boy or girl who leaves at 15 or 16.

What is needed, then, is one of two solutions to the problem. A reconstructed Youth Employment Service, very much larger than at present and staffed with well-trained vocational guidance experts, could second to the schools the officers who would do most of the work. A large four-stream grammar school would probably need almost the full-time services of such a person. He would interview pupils, discuss pupils with staff, meet parents and would have time to get to know the pupils as persons. There could always be someone available to give advice, from the career point of view, about the choice between subject options anywhere in the school, and to help the staff by keeping them up to date about certain important features of the outside world. The other solution moves a step further by following the American precedent of appointing, as a member of the school staff, someone trained in personal and vocational guidance. Such a person would ideally do a limited amount of teaching, perhaps as a member of the general studies team, and would play a part in some of the clubs and societies of the school. Each of these methods would provide a realistic career-guidance service. Until something like this can be achieved, the bulk of the work with sixth-formers will continue to be done by the school itself, though there will always be a need for vast quantities of information, and some mitigation of typical grammar school attitudes concerning particular careers. The obvious shortage of first-class applicants for careers in technology must be attributed, to some extent, partly to the ignorance and partly to the prejudices of some of those who advise sixth-formers. One could look to the vocational guidance office to bring to an end such a situation.

What must not be underestimated is the persistent need for advice of boys and girls when they are thinking of leaving school, especially when they have reached an educational level unknown to any member of their own families. They are entering an entirely new world, and it is obvious that in taking their first steps into it they will need a great deal of help. Whatever one does, one is conscious of the inadequacy of one's efforts, and there seems no end to the need for help and advice. There is little realisation on the part of local authorities or Ministry of Education of the urgency and seriousness of this great need, and Universities, professional bodies and employers are only slowly becoming aware of it.[1] Some sixth-formers are convinced that they are suited to a particular career: much hard work may have to be done to make sure that they understand its precise nature. What is a chemical engineer, how does he spend his time, and what are the qualities which bring success? What is the precise difference between courses in Bio-Chemistry, Bacteriology and Micro-Biology? What exactly is the job of a Production Engineer or a Municipal Engineer? Recent publications have been directed towards answering some of these and similar questions. Is it not time that all major professions followed the example of the British Medical Association, who in their pamphlet *Becoming a Doctor* have provided an admirable guide to the interested sixth-former? University departments might learn to give information simply and clearly, on the pattern of Nottingham University's leaflet *A Job Specification for a Chemical Engineer*. What is written must be aimed at the sixth-former and his parent; a semi-legalistic jargon is useless and information which is so skilfully hidden that only someone who already knows the answer can find it is of no great help. Easy access is essential to facts about courses, about possible careers which follow from them, and for the sixth-former who hopes to go directly into a post when he leaves school about the exact nature of that post and his prospects in it.

One of the exciting things which has been happening in the grammar school during the last decade has been a growth in the size of the sixth form, and a consequent lengthening of the school life of many pupils. In High Pavement School in 1954 there were 117 pupils: in 1963 the number had grown to 191. This same rapid increase is taking place throughout the country. It is due partly to the so-called 'bulge' in the birth-rate, but also because more and more parents and pupils are becoming convinced that a career in the sixth form leads effectively to better careers and positions of greater responsibility. The national statistics for pupils in sixth forms in all maintained schools in England and Wales are as follows: January, 1958, 76,279; January, 1959, 87,057; January, 1960, 99,214; January, 1961, 112,530; January,

[1] CRAC. Careers Research Advisory Centre of 25, St. Andrew's Street, Cambridge, now exists to develop and research into careers guidance.

1962, 121,669; January, 1963, 136,253. In maintained grammar schools during this time sixth form numbers have increased from 70,281 to 113,578. In January 1963 there were 53,554 pupils in the sixth forms of direct-grant and independent schools.

It is encouraging to find more and more first-generation grammar school children in the sixth form, and to find often that it is the children themselves who go home and tell their parents that they intend to stay at school until they are 18—in many cases parents who feel that they have made a great concession in allowing their son to stay until 16, and whose attitude to this new demand is one of half-resigned incredulity. Much recent research has shown that the proportion of children who stay into the sixth form whose parents are skilled or unskilled manual workers is still far below what it should be. The Robbins Report gives reasons for believing that more and more of these parents are beginning to demand a longer education for their children, especially sons, and this is supported by my own experience. Further, the Report expects this trend to continue, and bases much of its case for the rapid expansion of places in higher education on this expectation. Evidently some grammar schools are achieving success in their efforts to make themselves not unwelcoming to children whose relatives have had no experience of schools of this type. As schools learn to treat their sixth-formers increasingly as young men and women, and as local authorities realise that a large sixth form demands a very different type of provision from the rest of the school, the tendency to stay on will be strengthened. It is still true to say that far more boys than girls are staying on and there is much leeway to be made up in some parts of the country. In a good boys' school in a residential area not less than 75 per cent of the entry can be expected to enter the sixth form. At High Pavement School, which serves a mixed area of a different kind, about 60 per cent will do so.

There is every reason to believe, then, that sixth forms will continue to grow quickly during the next ten years. Comprehensive Schools are adding more to the number and the transfer of pupils who are taking O Level subjects in secondary modern and bi-lateral schools will increasingly swell the total. Staying on at school to 18 is rapidly becoming the accepted thing for the intelligent boy or girl. Many complaints are heard from employers because of their inability to attract the bright pupil who used to come to them at 16. Some professional bodies like bankers and accountants, once thought to be the impregnable stronghold of tradition, have faced facts and are actually preferring applicants with A Level passes. Dare we hope that we are within striking distance of the time when the grammar school course can be thought of as one lasting to 18, with only a comparatively few pupils dropping out at 16? Some bold local authority might even now ask the parents of a child who enters the grammar school to sign a contract to keep him there until 18, unless parent, school and authority agree that he should leave at 16. Surely the Leicestershire plan should make it particularly easy for this to take place.

It is a commonplace among heads of grammar schools that, during the last seven or eight years, the numbers of pupils wishing to go to University has increased far more quickly than the number of places which are available for them. Successive Ministers of Education and their advisers have consistently underestimated the demand for University expansion. It is now much more difficult for a pupil to obtain admission to a University than it was in 1957: the qualifications which easily obtained a pupil a place then are well below the standard required today, and we know that many of the students concerned more than justified their selection because the results of their degree examinations are available. This is part of the answer to those who still feel, in spite of Appendix One of the Robbins Report, that there are already too many University students, and that to admit more would necessitate a lowering of academic standards. One of the fascinating results of the debate about the Robbins Report has been some examination of the conception and function of a University in the life of this nation, in the second half of the twentieth century. Clearly there are still some who cling obstinately to the notion of a highly selective group of scholars, an intellectual élite engaged in pushing back the frontiers of knowledge. This conception would be suspicious of technological and vocational courses in Universities and would really prefer nothing but the special honours course in one of the orthodox academic subjects. Is it not clear that the needs of a highly complex modern society have already begun to dictate a modification of this view and will compel further rapid change as the twentieth century progresses? Nor will it be possible to ignore the demands for

University places of more and more young men and women who require University courses of a different nature. Grouped courses of the type which are being established at some of the newer Universities like Keele, Sussex, York and East Anglia, have an obvious attraction for students whose aim is not to become research students (as well as for some who will). Many existing courses in the more established Universities involve a combination of subjects for one or two years, a point which is often overlooked, and other University departments might with advantage ask themselves about the content of their courses and the way in which they are organised. One would expect a University to watch anxiously over the academic standard of its courses and its degrees: it is clearly its proper function to do so. But it is slightly absurd to find University dons pretending that these are objective standards, laid up in heaven, to which they alone have access. Grouped courses, involving vocational studies even, do not necessarily imply a lowering of standards. This is not to accept the view that a University place ought to be made available for every applicant who wishes to enter, regardless of ability: the problem of selection must remain. There is, however, a good case for saying that a place ought to be found somewhere in the field of higher education for almost all who want one.

The task of University selection is indeed a difficult one. As the number of applicants for each place in a particular department increases, the selecting body finds itself asking for higher and higher marks at A Level: magic numbers like 65, 65, 60 are demanded before a provisional offer of a place can be turned into a final offer. One University department, need one add that it is an Honours School in Mathematics, asked in 1963 for nothing less than two distinctions and a third A Level pass, which is surely a *reductio ad absurdum*. A Level, which was once thought of as a qualifying examination, is regarded as a finely graded sieve although, if we are honest, we must admit that it is the roughest of measuring rods. Apart from the selection of 'high flyers', who would presumably survive almost any conceivable selection machinery, the whole business has become a lottery which it is impossible to defend on rational ground. The system of conditional offers is on the verge of breaking down when applicants are frightened away from departments which ask for extravagantly high marks, and the departments obtain the just reward of empty places when the new academic year begins. Some departments in at least one University have found that, through skilful interviewing and a sensible use of school reports, it is possible to abandon the whole apparatus of provisional offers of places. The department finds that it can discover plenty of good candidates by making a qualifying offer: the candidates chosen need only obtain the two A Level passes which are necessary for matriculation purposes. In general, however, we have seen University entry turned into still another of the hurdles which our educational system spreads so generously in the path of a child from an unprivileged home. Perhaps we should modify the old conception of an educational ladder and in future use the metaphor of an obstacle race.

In the present highly competitive situation, however, those who have to select find that they have very little accurate information to guide them. A twenty-minute interview, usually conducted by untrained amateurs, can provide little but a highly subjective impression, and is no basis for scientific selection. The good University candidate is not a different sort of person from the inadequate one: a continuous spectrum of ability and personality factors is involved. Some reports from heads of schools are tremendously helpful, and where a department knows its schools well its selection is likely to be much more accurate, but it has to be confessed with shame that some heads are far from frank and their reports give no assistance. Examination results are hardly reliable as a test of university potential. Results at O Level are largely useless, and it is to be hoped that universities will cease to use them. A Level results are not available until the end of August, and those departments which rely on detailed marks have then to face a few hectic weeks during which the selection process has to be completed. There is a strong case for moving the A Level examination to March (or for starting the University year in January—while keeping O and A Level in the summer), and if O Level were taken at the same time a two-year A Level course could be maintained (and some of the nation's difficulties concerned with holidays might be solved). Even then it has to be remembered that A Level marks are subject to many factors like susceptibility to 'cramming' and differing qualities of teaching staffs and equipment, and cannot be regarded as an accurate prognostication of ability to do University work. A proper use of Special papers based on existing A Level syllabuses, but attempting to examine depth of thought, ability to use and understand generalisations and power of comprehension—instead of the capacity to learn and reproduce masses of information—might make the situation easier for University selectors. Without some more formal test of a candidate's capacity for further intellectual development, much of the selection must remain guesswork. One therefore welcomes the cautious reference in the Robbins Report to American experience in the field of objective testing for candidates for University entry. The Scholastic Aptitude Tests of the College Entrance Examinations Board (which has been steadily producing and improving its tests in the light of continuous research and of test results since 1926) and the American College Testing Program (Iowa City) which was organised in 1959, are two examples: it is a method which might certainly be experimented with in British conditions. The Robbins Report, in paragraph 232, recommends research in this country and refers to the large-scale experiment which is being tried in Scotland. One must express the hope that the unorthodoxy of this suggestion will not inhibit its use in the conservative atmosphere of British schools and Universities.

We can at least be thankful that circumstances have at last persuaded the Universities to accept some degree of centralised co-ordination in this field. The establishment of the Universities Central Council for Admissions (and it is ironical, and symptomatic, that it, too, in 1962 seriously underestimated the size of the problem with which it would be faced) has simplified the whole machinery of applications for University to the great advantage of all concerned. When the Oxford and Cambridge colleges, the London Medical Schools and the other institutions which have remained outside, have all joined in the scheme there should be in existence a rational system as far, at least, as the organisation of University admissions is concerned. A great advantage is that now, for the first time, it is possible to obtain accurate information about the number of boys and girls who are applying to universities, and about how many who are unsuccessful are academically qualified for admission.

In the first report of the Universities Central Council on Admissions, which covers the period 1961-3, valuable information is given. This is complete for Faculties of Technology in which the new system worked fully: in addition figures from a large sample of students applying to all other departments enable approximate numbers to be calculated. In all, it appears that about 10,000 applicants for university places with three A Level passes were unsuccessful and that of these about 1,750 obtained better than three grade D passes. In addition, more than 7,000 unsuccessful applicants emerged with two A Level passes. In fairness it must be added that approximately 60 per cent of these 17,000 applicants have continued in full-time education at school or elsewhere, presumably in an attempt to improve their qualifications. It is clear, however, that judged by the standards of the Robbins Report 17,000 qualified applicants applied for University places in 1962-3 and went empty away.

It would be absurd to suggest, of course, that all boys and girls who have obtained two A Level passes, and the appropriate passes at O Level, should necessarily go to University. To begin with, many have no wish to do so. Others would be unsuited to a University course because they are not really students, do not possess a desire to search after knowledge for its own sake, are not attracted by abstract ideas and do not wish to understand general principles. In attempting, very properly, to persuade pupils to stay into the sixth form, many schools have made use of the glamour of life at Universities: pupils have been attracted by their prestige without having much understanding of the implications of a University career. It is possible, therefore, to find among applicants for University, who have the appropriate academic qualifications, some who would be better advised to think of some other form of higher education.

School guidance has an obvious part to play in these matters and clearly some schools are failing in their duty. It is important that some candidates should be positively discouraged from making university applications, and heads of schools must say honestly in confidential reports if they have doubts about a particular candidate, or if they regard him as very much a borderline case. One recognises, of course, the difficulty of making an accurate prophecy, and I remember quite a number of cases in which events have proved me hopelessly wrong. Some boys have done far better than I ever thought possible, perhaps as a result of the stimulus of life and teaching at the University:

others have performed most disappointingly, for reasons which I have been unable to discover. In spite of all this, however, it is the duty of the head to give his sincere opinion, even if he turns out to be mistaken.

Beyond all this, the school must make a positive attempt to advise a pupil to choose that sort of higher education for which he is best fitted. This implies that the head (or whoever advises) must himself be well-informed about the great variety of opportunities which exists in higher education, and it must be admitted that some schools remain ill-informed. There are still teachers who know about Universities and Teachers Training Colleges, but are only just becoming dimly aware of Colleges of Advanced Technology. Some boys' schools do not positively encourage their pupils to enter Training Colleges. We need a final eradication of snobbish ideas about the superiority of one type of institution or one type of course. When we think of a C.A.T., we should not regard it as an institution which is suitable for those who are not quite good enough to win a University place, and it is quite clear that it has been so regarded in recent years. We should think of it rather as another type of University, but with a different purpose. Where the college is doing its job properly, it provides courses which are much more closely linked with industry and commerce than those of the University. Some of our pupils need this vocational and practical slant in their work, and it is a pity that the school itself fails to give it. We have all met pupils who are unable to realise their full potentiality until they can see the practical applications of their theoretical work, and the marriage of theory and practice in a course for a Diploma in Technology gives them precisely this, and one hopes that the Colleges of Advanced Technology will not attempt to imitate existing University courses in technology when they become technological universities. If, then, a boy is trying to make up his mind between a university course in Mechanical Engineering or a Diploma in Technology course in the same subject, the advice I should give him would be based on which course I think would suit him best, not on how much ability I think he has. We have to remember, too, that most Colleges of Advanced Technology include in their courses a considerable element of liberal studies, so conspicuously lacking from many University engineering courses (though the idea is beginning to spread). As soon as these Colleges are transformed into technical Universities and are included in the U.C.C.A. procedure, we shall see the end of absurd ideas about prestige. It is, perhaps, worth while to draw attention to the tremendous variety of courses in the Colleges, and to express the hope that effective advertisement and explanation of these courses will be undertaken.

In the discussion of the factors which induce the best sixth form scientists to choose pure rather than applied science, there are many points to be raised. Apart from the obvious fact that a pupil who is doing well in, and is tremendously excited by, Physics at school will naturally wish to continue studying this subject more deeply when he leaves, many sixth-formers are not at all clear at the age of 18 as to their ultimate career. A young scientist may only approach certainty as to the particular aspect of his subject which fascinates him most late on in his degree course. Is he then to commit himself, when he applies for admission to a University course at the age of 17, to some unknown application of his specialist subject? May he not be better advised to take a degree in a pure science and postpone a decision about the nature of the particular technology on which he will ultimately concentrate, until he is quite sure what he wants to do? It is much easier to convert himself from a pure into an applied scientist, after he has taken his degree, than it is to change from one application of a science to another. There is, too, some uncertainty in the mind of boys as to the availability of posts in a particular technology at some distant date in the future, and a boy might well feel it wise to retain as much mobility as he can for as long as he can.

The whole situation would, of course, be different if science teachers in the grammar school, especially those who were teaching sixth-formers, were well acquainted with the practical applications of what they were teaching and had some up-to-date experience in industry. An even greater need, however, is for a complete revision of A Level syllabuses in the Sciences and Mathematics, and it is encouraging that such revisions are being undertaken. A Modern Physics syllabus, or even better a carefully worked out Applied Physics or Applied Mechanics course, would introduce sixth-form scientists to aspects of science of which at the moment most of them are ignorant, and would put them in a position to make a far more realistic choice of a course when they enter higher education. Some Professors of Engineering in Universities must bear a share of responsibility for the present situation, since they have insisted that the schools should confine themselves to the pure Sciences and Mathematics, and should leave the introduction to technology to higher education. I am convinced that there will be no fair distribution of good sixth form scientists between pure and applied science courses in Universities and Colleges until sixth form science learns to pay some adequate attention to the application of scientific principles in the world outside. A number of grammar-technical schools have already shown what can be done in this field, and with considerable effect.

It has been suggested by those who do not wish to see a rapid expansion of the Universities, that there are many empty places in full-time degree courses in Technical Colleges, and that until these are filled it would be wrong to increase the number of places in Universities. Most of these courses are scientific, though some are concerned with the arts and social sciences and with commercial subjects. In addition, there are many part-time courses for Higher National Certificate, Higher National Diploma and the like. Frankly, part-time courses are inadequate if we are thinking of real higher education: obviously there are many boys and girls for whom these courses are suitable, but they cannot be regarded as a proper alternative to a university career. This particular method of obtaining a technical qualification has, with good reason, earned for itself the title of 'the hard way'. Full-time degree courses in a Technical College are a very different proposition and should certainly be considered seriously by a headmaster who is advising his pupils. Any headmaster, however, will wish to know a great deal about a technical college, its standards, its amenities and the quality of its communal life before he recommends his pupils to apply. In addition, a school must be satisfied that hostel accommodation or properly supervised lodgings are available for students who come from another town. Some of the best of the technical colleges have worked out courses which are first-class in all respects: others have staff of inferior quality and only mediocre facilities and equipment. If a technical college is a place which students attend for classes only, and where all concerned have a 'nine to five' philosophy, a headmaster will feel that his pupils are being fobbed off with something inferior. At the moment a good sixth form pupil will usually go to a technical college only if he has applied for and failed to obtain a place in a University. It will take a considerable time for knowledge to spread throughout the schools as to which colleges and courses should be avoided and which can be chosen quite happily. What many schools are looking for are colleges where they can be confident that the students will be thought of as persons who may have individual problems and needs for which someone in authority will have a real concern: it may, indeed, be added that not all University departments make convincing arrangements for the pastoral care of their students. If a technical college is to be thought of as a proper alternative to a University, it must attain certain obvious standards, and even bearing in mind the lower intellectual calibre of so many of their students one can only express alarm at the high rate of failure of students attempting degree courses in technical colleges. Similarly, there are excellent colleges of Art, Drama and Music, and others which are not so adequate not only academically but with regard to the considerations enumerated above. The schools will obviously prefer institutions which are able to offer not only continued training but also higher education in a full sense.

In this discussion of higher education establishments, Teachers Training Colleges have been left to the last. It may sound a truism to insist that entrants to these colleges should be intending teachers, and not persons who have failed to secure a University place and wish to continue their education, preferably with residence away from home. The training college is sometimes regarded as such a refuge, particularly by girls on the arts side who find its courses more attractive, and less demanding, than those of Universities. There is, indeed, a real need for another type of institution, intended particularly for arts sixth-formers, which may be described loosely as a Liberal Arts College. Many young men and women are not interested in an honours course of an academic type, but would prefer a broader course with a different objective, just as the College of Advanced Technology offers a differently based course on the science side. Obviously some excellent Teachers Training Colleges are already well able to develop quickly into Liberal Arts Colleges working in close connection with a University. If ever the happy day dawns when there is less pressure on the colleges to produce more and more teachers, one can conceive of a most valuable college dedicated to serve the educational needs of those who, in different professions, will deal with human beings, including teachers, youth club leaders, almoners, child-care officers and other social workers of all kinds.

The Robbins Committee has recommended and the government has agreed that a proportion of students in Teachers Training Colleges should be able to obtain University degrees. The degree should be a Bachelor of Education and should be an ordinary degree. The course might consist of three subjects, Education and two other subjects, and together with the normal college course is to occupy four years and at the end of this time a successful student will have both his degree and his teachers' certificate. Clearly there are numbers of students in these colleges who are well able to profit from such a course and there is no reason, apart from traditional notions as to what properly constitutes a degree course, why these students should be deprived of the opportunity. After all, it is already possible in various Universities to take degree courses in Education, Physical Education and Housecraft. Nor must it be assumed that teachers who obtain their degrees in Training Colleges will necessarily be those intending to teach in secondary schools: it is important that primary school teachers should be able to qualify for degrees in this way, and it would be quite wrong for the teaching profession to be divided into graduate and non-graduate teachers along the line of the split between secondary and primary schools. For these reasons, if no others, the degree course must be suitable for future teachers and must not be a slightly watered down version of an existing University syllabus, though naturally it must be such that the University can accept it as academically respectable. There is obviously here much room for negotiation, and one can imagine certain difficulties with some of the more orthodox and inflexible University departments.

Further recommendations of the Robbins Committee involve the creation of University Schools of Education, not accepted by the government in December 1964, and changes in the government and financing of the Training Colleges, or 'Colleges of Education.' The School of Education would take over the academic functions of the existing Institutes of Education and would consist of the University Education Department and the Colleges of

Education. The School should have its own academic board and subject boards of studies and the University subject departments would be represented on the latter. The degrees granted to college students would be degrees of the University, and the School of Education would be responsible to the University Senate for all the necessary procedures involved in the granting of degrees. The Colleges of Education themselves would be granted independent governing bodies, and the local education authorities would be no longer responsible for them, although they would be strongly represented on the boards of governors. The Colleges would be financed by ear-marked grants from the Universities Grant Commission, paid through the Universities to the Schools of Education. Disappointing though the government's refusal to accept these proposals is, it is quite clear that a policy of this sort would place the Training Colleges firmly within the sphere of higher education and give them the chance to grow in stature. It is encouraging that a few local authorities have recognised this fact, and have declared their willingness to see the Training Colleges on which they have lavished so much care and money become independent bodies in close association with a University. The great majority of local authorities, however, are opposing these proposals with all their strength, partly because they feel that they are unfair and partly because they feel it necessary to resist any reduction in their own powers. While it is true that most of the large local authorities have treated training colleges generously and have given them considerable independence, it must be recognised that a number of colleges have been prevented from achieving a proper development and expansion by local authorities. An institution which is to be expanded quickly, and is expected to do academic work of university standard, must be in a position in which it can substantially manage its own affairs and be free from the inhibiting control of what are often purely local considerations. After all, training colleges already recruit nationally, and their students go into schools which are scattered throughout the country: they have, in fact, outgrown the local connection which has done so much to build them up in the past.

The best Training Colleges are among the most lively and impressive educational institutions in the country, and are showing a capacity to think out new courses and to encourage new thinking about the traditional subjects which some University departments might emulate with advantage. On the other hand, there are still some which remain comparatively unaffected by this progressive spirit: there are, lamentably, even yet a few which treat their students as school children, and more in which college lecturers are much more likely to die in the last ditch in defence of their academic subject than in the interests of a student. One hopes that a rapid expansion in size and the recruitment of younger staff and more able students will soon blow away the remaining cobwebs. The training college has to face the problems not only of an unprecedented growth but also of the training of teachers in a quickly changing world. Changes in the content of the curriculum and in teaching methods can only come effectively through progressive training of teachers.

The Minister of Education announced in 1963 a much-needed expansion in the number of places in training colleges from 49,000 in 1962-3 to 65,000 in 1966-7 and 82,000 in 1970-1. At the same time he warned us that even in 1970 we should still be 35,000 teachers short. This decision was followed quickly by the Robbins Report which stated that these numbers were quite inadequate and recommended that in Colleges of Education in England and Wales there should be 110,000 places in 1973-4 and 131,000 places in 1980-1. The overall shortage of teachers at the moment is serious, and inside it there are particular shortages such as trained graduate teachers of Mathematics and Science among men, and shortages of well-qualified women graduates in almost all subjects. Ironically, these shortages exist at a time when University Education Departments have been turning away qualified candidates. In addition, in 1962, 2,000 qualified applicants were unsuccessful in applications to Training Colleges, almost half of those being regarded as good and acceptable candidates by the colleges. One can only welcome the belated conversion of the Ministry of Education to the need for a quick expansion: they have relied for too long, in spite of many warnings, on inadequate statistical information, and have pursued a complacent policy which has almost produced disaster. The teachers who were rejected were needed to educate the increasing numbers of children in the schools, which must produce a greater number of teachers to meet our future needs.

The headmaster of a grammar school is in an important strategic position in the education system. His task is to take the intelligent children from all kinds of homes, and to do his best to see that they receive an education which is suited to their particular talents. After all his labours, it is intolerable that he should see able children, who are fitted for University or training college, unable to find a place there. We talk of equality and opportunity and social justice, but we know that, at the moment, these things do not exist, nor will they in the foreseeable future; we know that thousands of children who are worthy of higher education do not even achieve a place in a grammar school because of the inadequacies of their social background; even when the grammar school helps a child to overcome these disadvantages, there may well be no place for him in University or training college. The national interest demands that the full potential of every child in the country shall be realised; the brains and personalities of the rising generation represent the most valuable investment which we can make as a nation. We can do full justice to persons and the best possible service to the community only if we are prepared to devote a far higher proportion of the national income to expenditure on education. Any government which is unwilling to take this responsibility seriously, or pays lip-service to it solely for the purpose of fighting a general election, is unfit to hold office. The state system must provide, for the children in its care, a standard of education which the best and wisest parents in the land insist upon for their own children.

I make no excuse for devoting the greater part of this chapter to higher education. It is clear that most grammar school pupils continue their education when they leave school, and as more and more stay on to 18 the tendency to enter full-time higher education will develop and accelerate. Among these pupils are many whose families had no previous contact with higher education, or with training for posts which involve the exercise of responsibility. Such young people have a particular claim on places in institutions for which they are fitted and on careers to which they aspire. The child from what is loosely called 'the uncultured home' has many obstacles to overcome. His parents can give him little but encouragement and moral support. He is adventuring in a new field and is competing against contemporaries whose parents know the moves and can play a major part in helping him to mature into a cultivated young man. As

I have indicated earlier, he may still be suffering from a degree of inarticulacy, or may have escaped partially from it into a condition of rather crude and brash argumentativeness. He is likely to have feelings of insecurity in his social relationships and to lack poise and *savoir-faire*. Yet beneath all this, he may be far more mature in fundamentals than the assured young man from the independent boarding-school and the well-to-do middle-class background.

What is likely to happen to such a candidate when he is interviewed for a place at a University? This depends very much on the personality and skill of the interviewer. If the interview is formal in tone, if no successful attempt is made to make effective human contact with the candidate, he is unlikely to feel comfortable enough to express himself freely and to do himself justice. Still worse, he may in desperation become aggressive and give the impression of a brash uncultivated teenager. Many boys and girls fail to get across their interest in or even their excitement about their studies, because the atmosphere of the interview is unsympathetic. Many interviews fail because of a comcomplete lack of communication. One hears the occasional almost unbelievable report from a boy who returns from an interview. One very sensitive young man was conscious throughout of a highly hostile atmosphere, and had to listen to two members of the interviewing panel discussing his accent and speech in a very critical manner. This young man came back depressed and defeated, and it was hardly surprising that he was most reluctant to face the risk of a second similar experience.

A more serious difficulty is competition with a socially confident boy from an independent school for a place in an Oxbridge College, or for entry to Dartmouth or Sandhurst. One has been told, on many occasions, that the interviewers 'fall over backwards' to be fair to the grammar school boy: it is, however, a matter of observation that only a small number of the places at Dartmouth and Sandhurst are filled by grammar school boys, and many Oxbridge dons bemoan the fact that only a few such boys obtain admission to their colleges unless they win open scholarships. I have not the slightest doubt that the people who interview have every intention of being fair and are far from allowing class feeling to influence their decisions. The real difficulty is much more subtle: it lies in the fact that many of the

144

interviewers are pre-disposed by their own education and upbringing to recognise the best qualities which can be found in
the boy from their own sort of background. What they are
rarely qualified to do is to detect beneath the reticent and rather
gauche manner of the grammar school boy, who is operating in
formidable and unfamiliar surroundings, his valuable qualities,
his maturity which is different in kind from that of his rival,
and above all his potentiality. To do this successfully demands a
degree of sympathetic understanding which is most likely to be
found in someone whose own personal experiences have been
similar. Some years ago the head of a Cambridge college, who
insisted on seeing applicants for the first time when they were 16
wrote to me about one of them, 'I find that I simply do not
understand him: I am quite unable to get into communication
with him'—and anyone who knew the master concerned could
hardly be surprised. While, then, interviews are frequently conducted by the products of the 'establishment' schools and background, it seems likely that, with the best will in the world, the
qualities which they look for will be found most easily in boys
from the same backgrounds as themselves. It must in justice be
added that many Oxbridge colleges are seriously concerned because they admit so few boys from under-privileged homes and
schools. A system which appears to tolerate or perpetuate social
injustice is hardly likely to last long in the second half of the
twentieth century. Those few colleges which maintain methods
of selection which are not open to the light of day, and which
are based upon the predilections of an individual don for potential 'blues' or members of certain families or schools, would be
well advised to reconsider their methods.

The great prestige of Oxford and Cambridge produces serious
and disturbing effects on selection for university places. These
universities still attract a very high proportion of the most intelligent products of the schools, and their open scholarships are
regarded as the highest prize which English education can offer.
As a result, these scholarships exercise an unfortunate influence
on sixth form curricula and can be counted one of the most
potent causes of excessive specialisation. In this field again,
highly selective schools (which, obviously, include some of the
independent boarding-schools) have a very great advantage.
Their whole sixth form system can be geared to open scholar-

ships: boys can, in effect, begin to prepare for them at 16. In the ordinary maintained grammar school only a tiny minority of boys will enter for the scholarship, and the identity of these may not be known until A Level has been taken. The school, then, has to choose between two policies, unless, indeed, it decides to have nothing to do with the wretched business. It can either allow the fact that a few boys may wish to take an open scholarship to influence the treatment of a substantial proportion of sixth-formers, or it must allow the small number of boys concerned to take their chance after a preparation for the scholarship which lasts about three months. It is hardly surprising that the independent and large direct-grant schools win a high proportion of the open scholarships, especially when one takes into account their smaller classes, their better-paid teaching staffs and the usually superior social backgrounds of their pupils. However, the genuine 'high flyer' in the maintained schools, who has not been 'creamed off' into one of the more selective institutions, can be sure that his ability will win him an award, regardless of his social background. For this reason some heads of grammar schools support the continuation of the open scholarship system. Others, however, and this writer is one of them, deplore their evil effects on the curriculum of the sixth form, and their contribution to the excessive competition for entry into these two universities. A concentration within two universities of a high proportion of the nation's talent can only be brought about at the expense of the other universities.

One looks forward, therefore, to a speedy abolition of open scholarships, accompanied by the entry of the Oxbridge colleges into the U.C.C.A. Scheme. It is interesting that, in 1963-4 some colleges reported a considerable reduction in the number of applications for places. There are still many boys in maintained grammar schools who are unwilling to stay in the sixth form for a third year, and if the ancient universities wish to attract some of these they must accept the admission scheme which is common to all universities. How they will select them remains a mystery. Until they can improve their selection techniques, the only suggestion one can make is that a college should cease to make entry competitive between candidates from maintained grammar schools and independent schools and should apply some sort of unofficial rationing scheme.

## Leaving School

The last few years have been notable for a rapid increase in the number of Colleges of Further Education which provide part-time and full-time courses in a tremendous range of subjects. In many areas these colleges have shown impressive enterprise and initiative and their amazing success is proved by the speed with which their courses have become over-subscribed. Together with the technical colleges they offer magnificent opportunities in both vocational and general education. It is important that there should be a close collaboration between the schools and the colleges, so that each shall understand what the other is attempting to do, and that senior pupils in the schools become aware of the rich variety of educational opportunities which awaits them. Unfortunately, in some areas, an element of rivalry has grown up when the colleges have introduced A Level courses, as it is perfectly proper for them to do where there is a demand for them. It is a pity, however, when colleges not only duplicate courses which already exist in schools but use them to attract students away from sixth forms: in these cases personal discussion and co-operation between principals and heads seem necessary, though it is obvious that the difficulty is less likely to arise when sixth forms offer happy personal relationships and efficient teaching. Surely the work of these institutions should be complementary rather than competitive, and one hopes to see sixth-formers on part-time release to the colleges to take courses which the school is unable to provide, and it ought not to be impossible for the reverse process to take place. For example, it is difficult for any but a very large grammar school to offer A Level courses in all the main modern languages, and here is an opportunity for a college of further education or a technical college to help all the schools in an area. The engineering course at High Pavement School was one which could not have existed without half-day release of sixth-formers to Nottingham Technical College. The education of children after they have reached the age of 15 is an activity which involves institutions of different sorts and with varied approaches and methods: none of these has a monopoly of wisdom, and it is clear that they should all be working closely together. How often have I known a boy who has been a comparative failure academically at school, blossom forth and develop quickly in work and personality when he has left school, gone into the outside world and

continued his education in a new environment and with a different objective. No educational institution, no matter how efficient
or concerned with the welfare of its students it may be, can
expect to be equally successful with them all and it must not
be offended if some of them flourish better in a different climate.

It would be quite unrealistic, in a chapter on Leaving School,
not to refer to the recommendations of the Robbins Committee
concerning the number of places which should be made available
in the next twenty years in higher education. In spite of Appendix One of the Report there are still some who doubt if the vast
numbers of students will be forthcoming from the schools. How,
they ask, will it be possible to produce by 1973-4 179,000 university students, 110,000 students in Teachers Training Colleges and
45,000 in Further Education, 335,000 in all in England and Wales
(as compared with 108,000 university students, 49,000 in Training Colleges and 28,000 in Further Education, making 185,000
in 1962-3). The figure of 481,000 for 1980-1 is even more startling.
However, the statistical information in the Robbins Report is
very difficult either to repute or to ignore, taking account as it
does of the variations in the number of 18-year-olds, and of estimates both of the proportion of the age-group likely to reach a
level of attainment suitable for entry into higher education, and
of the proportion likely to apply for entry. The Report itself
points out that their numbers do not imply a lowering of the
standards needed to obtain places, nor do they assume a great
increase in the proportion of girls entering higher education
(which might well come about).

The Ministry's statistics for 1962 show that since 1954 there
had been a 72 per cent increase in the number of school leavers
with 5 or more O Level passes, and an increase or more than 100
per cent in the number with 2 or more A Level passes. Part of
this increase was due to the larger age-groups in the schools, but
if allowance is made for this the increases are 44 per cent and
75 per cent respectively. There is every reason to assume that
this growth in the size of sixth forms will continue, since more
and more parents are becoming convinced of the value of a sixth
form career. As this conviction spreads through the less-privileged
classes in the community, the demand for places in the sixth
form and in higher education will expand, and we may eventu-
ally find that the projections in the Robbins Report are an under-

estimate. Recent research among educational sociologists, supported by the experience of innumerable teachers, shows that where parents believe intensely in the value of the education which their children are receiving there is a strong likelihood that the children will have a successful career. We are witnessing a revolutionary change in the educational expectations of the parents of many English children—a change which is coming about as their standard of living improves and as they become the heirs of an affluent society.

# 9

# *Culture and the Grammar School*

TRADITIONALLY, EDUCATION has been concerned with the task of cultural transmission and the culture in question has been that of a minority group. It has been the duty of the schools to preserve this culture—the best that has been thought and said—and to hand it on reverently, to an élite class. During the twentieth century, this élite has rapidly increased in size, and the grammar school in particular has extended its influence into new areas of society. For years, too, it has been becoming apparent that in a highly concentrated and technological society, new conceptions of the function of education must replace the old. The schools can no longer confine themselves to the business of handing on an unchanged or even a slowly changing body of information and attitudes. Education, in the second half of the twentieth century, must be prepared to help in the process by which culture changes and develops and, in addition, must face the difficult and complicated task of spreading it throughout society. In the past, people who inherited or achieved a certain position in society were able to procure a worthy education for their children: today, through education, the children of the poor may rise socially and secure for themselves a training, and therefore a career, which assures them of a place in society.

Rapidity of change in our complex modern society must be reflected in changes in the content of education. Can anyone doubt this who has seen the coming of radio and television, the dawning of automation, the arrival of space travel and of the age of the motor-car? To put it at its lowest, the individual must be prepared to live in a quickly changing world which makes demands on him which are very different from those he would have had to meet a generation ago. An 'establishment culture' with its eyes firmly fixed on the past and unable to respond to modern developments in society and the arts—and a time-lag of approximately one generation is typical of the cultural responses to be expected in this quarter—can play no effective part in the lives of young people who are growing up today. Their choice will not be between the culture of the establishment and what has been described earier as the culture of the intelligentsia, it will rather be between the latter and 'pop culture'. For the school is not the only cultural agency which has to be taken into account. Family, the Church for a minority, mass communications, young people's organisations and the whole teenage sub-culture compete with the schools in influencing the young. These tremendously strong influences will work, quite often, in a direction which is quite contrary to that which the schools prefer. In such circumstances, to give the impression that culture is something which happened in the past, something which has stood the test of time, is to convince young people that culture is out of date, and the education which aims to transmit it is equally old-fashioned. In any case, if you cannot appreciate the cultural developments which are taking place around you, there must be something undeveloped about you. This is not to say that everything which is happening now must automatically be better than what is handed down from the past, but it would be remarkable if nothing which has been produced in the last thirty years is worthy of your august notice.

It has often been said that the greatest danger before our society is a split between an educated, 'cultured' and privileged minority and a semi-educated, 'uncultured' and under-privileged majority —and the appearances are that we are heading for such a situation. If this be true, it must be recognised that there is no prospect of diffusing throughout society what has been called above the culture of the establishment—the official arts and sciences, the conventional political and social attitudes, the typical religious and moral conceptions which are accepted by the powers that be. The cultural gulf can only be filled if culture is thought of quite differently, and it follows that the schools must be concerned with cultural innovation as much as cultural transmission. To concentrate on what are called typically the 'fine arts' is to court defeat: to assume that pure science has at last achieved a condition of respectability, while science which is applied (and is therefore presumably impure) remains outside the cultural fold is to combine an odd form of snobbery with an invitation to economic disaster. Culture must not be thought of as a decoration which dignifies those who are fortunate enough to possess it. It is far wider and much more fundamental; it must be concerned with the conceptions upon which society is based, the basic way of life.

The grammar school stands at the meeting point in society of the two cultures, the élite of whichever kind and the mass. Its connections with the university, its traditional role of preparing its pupils to enter an educated class, which has now been extended to cover thousands of children from under-educated homes, make its position both crucial and extremely difficult. As has been pointed out, there are many who feel that the grammar school is unfitted by its historical alliance with the middle-classes to broaden its sphere of influence among children who come from what are thought of as working-class homes. There are those who feel, for this and other reasons, that the grammar school has outlived its educational usefulness and must be replaced by the comprehensive school. It is clear that public opinion has come to condemn selection by the procedures known popularly as the 11-plus, and there are many who think that 11 is too young. It is still not clear, however, that public opinion is convinced that the comprehensive school is the universal answer, even though a comparatively small number of such schools, as a *tour de force*, may be able to achieve a great success. Throughout the country local authorities are trying different experiments in the organisation of secondary education. The Leicestershire plan, by which parents decide if they wish their children to pass into the grammar school at 14 with a comprehensive school before that age, is growing in popularity in slightly different forms. Bi-lateral schools, with duplicate G.C.E. streams in secondary modern schools and transfer to grammar school sixth forms at 16, represent only one way of organising overlapping courses which make selection provisional rather than final. The three-tier system of schools, which introduces a middle school between 9 and 13 and allows parents then to choose a grammar school if they wish, is beginning to make progress and is thought by many to offer the best hope for the future. Still another scheme would place all children of 11 to 16 in a comprehensive school and transfer all who wish to a sixth form college. The advantage of plans of this kind is that no major building developments are involved; in contrast to a system of comprehensive schools, they can be accommodated very largely in existing buildings. Even where entirely new building is envisaged, there are a number of authorities who are adopting the 'campus' plan in which secondary schools of different types occupy the same site, sharing some facilities and working closely together to ensure ease of transfer of pupils from one to the other.

It seems unlikely that a Labour government will bring into existence a compulsory plan which will make comprehensive schools universal: it is far more likely that different local authorities will adopt different solutions which fit circumstances and educational aspirations in their own areas. Much educational opinion is unwilling to write off the secondary modern school as a failure, especially since it has been in existence for such a short time; many believe that, in the area in which it has developed its own expertise, it can perform its cultural task at least as effectively as the comprehensive school, given proper conditions and equipment. It is conceivable that a good grammar school and a good secondary modern school, complementing each other and with much overlapping and complete ease of transfer, can together do their duty to society in a manner which will be socially acceptable. The notion that a child should enter an appropriate school or course may well, given time, replace the conception of selection and parents' choice that of direction.

Two things at least are clear: the first that the grammar school, in one form or another, is likely to go on existing, the second that the cultural problem with which this book is largely concerned must be solved whichever school system is adopted. The reorganisation of a system of schools, of itself, solves few educational problems, and our present pre-occupation with machinery may well be getting in the way of a much more fundamental and much more necessary reform of the school curriculum.

If, then, the grammar school will continue to exist, what can we say about its particular problems? The influx of first-generation pupils must be faced honestly in all grammar schools, as it has already been faced in many. This is no temporary problem which is with us only for a generation; it will last for the rest of the century and will become more, rather than less, difficult as more children from under-privileged homes enter its doors. The achievement of even a theoretical equality of opportunity will depend on a change in the attitude of parents, especially those in the lower income groups. There is unmistakable evidence that parental attitudes and expectations determine to a large extent the effectiveness with which their children can be educated. A verbally restricted home background will inhibit a child's progress at school: if his parents know and care nothing about education, the possibility of a real educational development is almost denied to him. Where a parent wishes his child to 'get on' educationally, even when he cannot give any assistance himself, there is a real hope that something can be done. The experience of the last twenty years has taught us that, as the skilled working classes have become increasingly affluent, their educational aspirations and expectations for their children have approximated more and more closely to those of the middle classes—hence the great increase in the size of the sixth form and the acute competition for places in universities. The spread of these notions throughout that large group in society which used to be described as lower middle class and upper working class is by no means complete and will continue during the next decade. The problem of the children of the unskilled and only partly skilled worker remains very largely to be tackled. The evidence which we possess leads us to expect that the distribution of intelligence in this area of society is likely to be similar to the distribution elsewhere. In other words we must assume the existence of thousands of children who could profit from education in a grammar school and at university. Before this pool of ability can be tapped, great changes will be needed in housing and town planning, there must be an appreciable improvement in standards of living, and as a product of all this changes in parental attitudes and expectations as far as the education of their children are concerned. *Education and the Working Class* suggests that educational equality of opportunity can be brought about by a change in the organisation of secondary education. This is a superficial view which over-simplifies a subtle and complex social problem. The achievement of a complete education of the entire population can come about only at the end of a long process of social change. At the moment, we are in the middle of this change, which may be accelerated if far-sighted social policies are adopted. Educational change comes, largely, as a result of social change; of itself, it can only help in the process of change in society and only then if it is working in the same direction.

At this moment in time the educational needs of the more intelligent pupils, whether they are to be found in a comprehensive school, a sixth form college or a grammar school, and bearing in mind the rapidly changing social composition of the group, must differ in important respects from what they were in 1930. This is not to overlook some of the values which could be derived from the old academic curriculum—the ability to study, the stamina and perseverance, the willingness to struggle against and overcome difficulties. One hopes that these will be developed in the future as in the past, but as they stand they do not make an attractive or heartwarming offer to the student who is new to the grammar school. This type of pupil, even more than most others, needs much personal nourishment; he will respond convincingly if he is aware of the relevance of what he is doing, and there is a great need to pay attention to his particular motivation. In a quickly changing technological society, education will be effective only if those in charge bear constantly in mind the importance of relevance and the motivation of their pupils, as well as their perpetual need for personal nourishment.

One particular danger which the grammar school faces today, as Bantock has pointed out, is that in combination with the university it will produce 'a rootless, socially mobile intellectual' who is narrowly specialised and uninterested in leisure-time 'cultural' activities. Have we, indeed, foreseen realistically the amount of leisure which many people will have—one hardly dare say enjoy—by the end of the century? The results of techno-logical progress, the spread of automation, the use of computers are all gradually increasing the quantity of leisure time which is available for many of our fellow-citizens. Who dare prophesy what will be the effect on life in the nineteen-seventies and eighties of the changes which are now on the drawing-board and in the laboratory. In the face of all this, who will deny the crying need for an education in leisure and for the nourishment of the whole man. We can hardly reconcile ourselves to a situation in which more people spend still more time passively watching television, submerged in pop music, reading cheap magazines, achieving the intellectual heights of bingo or even aimlessly consuming alcohol. What we should be interested in will be pursuits which contain within themselves the possibility of further development, so that a youth's interests and tastes do not atrophy at the age of 16 and leave him stunted for life. Many young people already have such interests which may include jazz, travel, sport, design, the modern novel, politics, the applications of science and films; in each of these can surely be found a growing-point which the school can nourish and help to develop into a meaningful use of leisure. If the school can do its job properly, starting with the interest which is already there and not with one which is completely remote from the experience of its pupils (for example, Bach or Shakespeare), many young persons will grow beyond the stage when entertainment is their sole aim, to a point at which it is possible to appreciate one of the arts (which is not to say that beween art and entertainment there is a deep gulf fixed). When they leave school one wants them to be in the middle of a development which is bound to continue, so that whichever art it may be can exercise its enriching effects on the human spirit. The continued neglect of the arts and crafts, in many boys' grammar schools, amounts to a crying scandal; a great and positive effort is imperative while the pupil is passing through the school if the opportunity is not to be missed, perhaps for ever. The notion still apparently exists in some schools, even among the staff, that manliness implies philistinism in the arts and that it is impossible for a rugby player to paint a picture. Whatever the pupil likes, he must be helped to an appreciation of the best of that type; what is most needed is an education in making choices—in discrimination.

Closely connected with education in the use of leisure is the positive need for a training to play a part as a valuable member of a democratic community. This implies a knowledge of and an interest in the working of the political system, and a willingness, even a determination to participate fully. Democracy demands a great deal of the individual citizen, that he should be well-informed, be willing voluntarily to sacrifice his time for the benefit of all, that he should be tolerant of minorities and able to recognise that his fellow-citizens have equal rights with himself. Beyond this, he should make an effective personal contribution to society whether as scientist, accountant, bus conductor or miner. If he is concerned with industry, at any level, he should be moved by a conception of industry as a public service and not merely as a means to private prosperity. Such an outline of the civic and social virtues draws attention at once to the neglect of this kind of education in many schools, where it appears that pupils are expected to pick up desirable attitudes magically from the general atmosphere of the school, or at any rate from their own homes. An understanding of the political life of ancient Athens, or of the issues involved in the English Civil War, is assumed to be an effective preparation for citizenship in this country in the twentieth century: it may perhaps be suggested mildly that the principle of relevance might be applied.

It is in the sphere of education towards the development of personal values, not only social but also moral and religious, that the school experiences its greatest difficulty, though there are few who would deny that this is a most important part of its activities. The strong disagreements in the world outside, the appearance of an almost complete abandonment of standards in a hectic search for material advancement and entertainment at all costs, combined with what must seem to many pupils the utter irrelevance and unreality of the values, no doubt sincerely held, of those in authority in school, together make the efforts of the school seem often futile and unconvincing. Agreed syllabuses and the survival in the schools of conventional religious attitudes, with which many pupils have no contact in their lives apart from school, serve to make the problem almost insoluble. And yet it is imperative that growing boys and girls shall be helped to acquire standards and values of their own, and shall not be left without help and guidance in a confusing and often unprincipled adult society. Here the school and the teacher have the plain duty to try to understand the pupil in his actual situation, however difficult that may be. Children must be challenged by the discussion of what constitutes the good life, with its implications of a respect for the integrity of others and a corresponding self-discipline from ourselves. After all, many ordinary imperfect men and women are attempting to live a reasonable moral life and it must be the object of the school to add to their number.

Whenever the school is concerned with values and attitudes, no matter whether they are aesthetic, civic, ethical or religious, the greatest sin lies in an attempt by the teacher to impose those which he holds himself. The most valuable and the most lasting convictions are those which we work out for ourselves. We can be helped to do this by a sympathetic person who has been through the same process himself. We may even come to share his convictions if we come to them in our own way and in our own time. If he attempts to use authority, superior knowledge or intelligence to impose them on us either he will drive us into complete opposition or he will cow us into a lukewarm acceptance of what we are told. In the latter case, it is hardly possible to think of the result as real convictions which can form a basis for action. The results of unwise attempts at missionary activities in school are to be seen around us. The teacher no longer has the social prestige he once possessed; in any case, his values have to compete with those the child meets in his own family and neighbourhood, in the adolescent sub-culture and the mass media. An attempt at conversion, indoctrination, the imposition of a superior culture is both mistaken and educationally indefensible. The object must be to help the pupil to achieve his own standards; the teacher's mind and personality are properly used as a whetstone on which the growing child can sharpen his wits and test his attitudes. Many teachers find this process both wearing and difficult. It is much easier to deliver yourself once and for all of a description of the standards you know to be right. Some find close contact with jejune, critical and rather arrogant adolescents almost too infuriating to be borne, and if this is the case they should not be allowed to teach them. On the other hand, the influence of a sympathetic and understanding teacher, who knows when to be patient and when to be astringent, can work wonders even with the most captious young man.

We should not wish to find the 18-year-old saying 'the right thing', having accepted uncritically the views and standards of his teachers and his parents. He should be in the middle of a continuous development with an ability to continue growing, which implies that he can change his views in the light of his changing and developing experience. There is often a genuine hostility between the adolescent and the adult world which has to be accepted. How much better that the adolescent should have the opportunity to work through this stage in the friendly atmosphere of a school where those in authority are sensitive and mature enough to understand just what process is taking place under their eyes. What a betrayal it is when the school remains unconcious of the problem and blunderingly adopts the authoritarian attitude. Need it be said that it is particularly stupid for a school to be hostile to the 'pop culture' of the adolescent, a policy which almost disqualifies it from being able to participate fully in a genuine education. Whether we like it or not—and many teachers definitely do not—our time is one in which values are changing, and we must expect the change to continue at an accelerating pace. It would be wrong then to educate our pupils as if values were static and as if all the answers were known, once and for all. On the contrary, we must educate for progress and development in standards while giving our pupils access to the best which has been handed down from the past.

The curriculum of the grammar school, at the moment, leaves little space for the sort of education which we have been discussing. It is concerned with a much more remote and academic kind of learning, which is not obviously based on the needs of, or an understanding of, the society which exists. Much of it seems almost calculated to repel intelligent children, and it is no secret that many of them are at times acutely bored. This is a great pity, since the first-generation child has a particular need to be reconciled to a comfortable reception of ideas and knowledge which are outside the range of his home background. He has to be persuaded to co-operate willingly in the process, and he will be helped to do this if what he is studying seems relevant. After all, this attempt to teach an understanding of important principles—whether scientific or in the field of historical development or of literary criticism—can equally well be made through subject matter and areas of human activity which appear relevant to the pupil, or remote from and out of touch with reality as he knows it. If, in addition, he is submerged in a sea of boring detail, which has to be learned apparently solely for the benefit of the external examiner, it is fair to bring up the question of motivation. Is it reasonable to offer as the sole motive for effort the hope of success in a distant examination?

Indeed, the grammar school and its competitors must make a gigantic effort to throw off their examination chains. There can be little doubt that O Level stands in the way of a much needed reform of the curriculum. It once had the important object of bringing about a much needed raising of academic standards, but its usefulness has now been outlived and it has become, in addition, a major reason for the boredom and even hostility of many pupils. While these lines were being written, it was most heartening to find the Secondary School Examinations Council, even belatedly, exposing the futility of O Level English Language examinations. Nor can the suggestion be tolerated that, without O Level, work in the main school will become flabby, that standards will be lowered, and that the entire fabric of the English educational system will collapse. Could defeatism in the teaching profession be pushed farther? On the contrary, it will at last be possible for teachers to choose syllabuses and adopt methods which will be aimed at developing the capacity to think rather than to recapitulate, to solve problems rather than to retain information. There will also be more time for the inclusion of educationally valuable material which is now excluded by examination pressures. What is needed is the abolition of O Level, the acceptance of the principle that a grammar school course normally ends at the age of 18, and the use of the Certificate of Secondary Education for the minority who must leave at 16. This will allow the emergence of a new pattern of teaching and experiment with a wide range of new techniques and teaching aids.

When we come to Advanced Level, we must face the need for a continuing revision of syllabuses, and a reduction in their extent, aimed at the substitution of a deepening understanding for a superficial knowledge of a wide area (most needed, for example, in Chemistry). If A Level passes become only a qualifying standard for university entrance, and special papers based on the same syllabuses but of a different kind are used for selection purposes, sixth form work, too, can be relieved of a considerable part of its examination burden. There will be room for liberally conceived and well-planned general studies courses which can remove the ill effects of specialisation. Experiments in continuous assessment with internal marking combined with external moderation, and based on syllabuses chosen by the school and accredited externally, must lead, sooner or later, to a situation in which education replaces examinations as the chief priority in the life of the sixth-former. We have, indeed, suffered far too long from a self-imposed examination machinery which amounts to a great industry, complete with many vested interests. How much better they order these things in France! One looks forward to the time, surely close at hand, when the curriculum of the grammar school will be freed from much of this external pressure. Refurbished and with an entirely new look, it will do a far better job than it has ever done, in developing the intellectual powers, broadening the interests and enabling the personalities to grow of the intelligent children who are its members.

Once the burden is removed a complete change in methods of teaching becomes possible; subservience to examination requirements has caused a concentration on individual progress, on frequent testing, on competition between one pupil and another. Indeed, if a pupil helps his friend accusations of dishonesty usually follow. If it is true that membership of a chosen group is particularly important to children from the less privileged homes, would it not be well to allow such children the opportunity to experience success in a group? Many school groups offer means of self-realisation, whether through participation in scouts, an orchestra, a play or helping old-age pensioners; this kind of creative activity often helps the individual to grow more effectively than any amount of individual competition. The same principle can surely be used inside the classroom. In history, a period can be studied in depth when groups of three pupils, acting as research teams complete with writer, illustrator and researcher, concentrate on different aspects of the period; a synthesis of their efforts completes the work, and an exhibition can be held of work to which everyone has contributed and parents and the whole school can come to see it. Similarly, in English Literature, given a large room with a stage, an entire class can be occupied in the task of acting, producing, lighting, dressing and stage managing a play with a public performance to conclude. In science, research teams have an obvious place in the solution of problems. Team teaching, which combines lecturing to a large class with small tutorial and seminar classes, must lead to the development of different techniques, and can bring effectively into use teaching machines and audio-visual aids. Individual progress, competition, frequest testing and external examination can recede into the background. By newer methods the pupil can progress at his own speed, helped by those around him—both teachers and pupils—responding in his own way and developing his own interests. The curriculum can become more immediate and more relevant, facts are discovered in order to be used and the boredom and frustration which are involved in the school life of most pupils can be minimised. Is a boy in a C form guilty of moral failure because he reacts differently from an A boy? Is it not imperative that each pupil must have experience of success, if his membership of the school is to have meaning for him and if he is to grow as a person? Need we organise our schools on the basis that approximately 40 per cent of our pupils will 'fail' in a particular subject at the age of 16?

What must the attitude of the grammar school be, if it is to be properly receptive to children of under-educated parents? R. S. Peters has referred somewhere to the fact that the task, rather than the teacher, should exert authority; if the pupil is engaged in activities which he enjoys, most problems of discipline disappear. In general, the school and those in authority in it must be receptive, permissive and liberal, concerned to minimise the contrast between the standards of home and school. This certainly implies some understanding of the nature of the home and close relations between parents and staff. There should be a willingness at school to re-examine the validity of long-standing assumptions about appearance, accent and good manners. Any teacher who can use the word 'common' with reference to pupils should be excommunicated on the spot. Throughout the educational process, an act of imagination is required which will enable the teacher to think himself into the background of the newcomer, and it may well be easier for him to do this if he was himself a first-generation grammar school pupil. Personal contacts with pupils, and personal knowledge of the individual, provide the best foundation for a helpful and warm relationship which can help a pupil through the complex stage of self development which ought to be taking place while he is at school, and this must include a growth in articulateness—a special problem in itself. Tensions between home and school there will be, but there is no reason at all why a first-generation grammar school child should find it impossible to be very happy either in his school or at home. Thousands have managed this with little difficulty. They have found that in some respects they have grown beyond their parents, but there are still many areas of common experience and many parents can go some part of the way with their children. The fact has to be faced, however, that in one sense the acquisition of real education implies a separation from home and neighbourhood though it need not be a painful process; many parents have the good sense to expect it to happen, indeed they may wish it to happen; after all, some neighbourhoods are better escaped from if the process of development is to be at all possible, and here the school has an even more difficult task which needs a sensitive and delicate understanding of the individual pupil and his circumstances.

Many children from what is loosely called a working-class background bring with them qualities which should certainly be preserved. I include here an unwillingness to be impressed by what is pretentious, a sturdy self-respect which finds it difficult to accept an authority which is insensitive to a person's feelings and rights, a healthy scepticism, a capacity, indeed, a strong desire to work happily with a group. These attitudes are valuable in themselves and should be integrated with the civilised qualities which we expect in a grammar school. Personal aggressiveness, intolerant criticism, crude argumentativeness must be accepted, lived with and sometimes even enjoyed, as a necessary stage in the growth of some children who come from an inarticulate and under-educated home. The school has to act as a bridge between the world of the educated and the environment of the child; this bridge must be a broad and comfortable way, with gentle gradients and free from obstacles.

There is then no reason why a reformed grammar school should be unable to offer the kind of atmosphere in which children from all kinds of backgrounds can be happily at home together. Many schools have proved this already, others are changing very quickly, and in almost all there are some teachers who have grasped the realities of the situation. A synthesis of what is best in the attitudes of working-class and middle-class homes is within the reach of all who wish to achieve it. We must certainly avoid making these new recruits to education more establishment than the establishment itself. One can perhaps envisage the gradual reform even of Oxbridge as a result of the infiltration of this newer type of undergraduate who is sceptical of the value of much which is to be found there. It is possible to

163

enjoy good architecture, good food and wine without necessarily accepting all that goes with it. All universities, indeed, might benefit if the first-generation student could bring with him some of his intense realism. Society has to earn its living through industry and technology; it is unfortunate that some university attitudes remain still unwilling to recognise this fact. Certainly the grammar school might do well by society if it produced a group of young people who are not impressed by mere financial success, who see industry as a social service, profitability as not the only test of efficiency and who are more concerned with quality of life than quantity of possessions.

The suggestion has been made elsewhere in this book that grammar schools have, in the past, attempted to keep themselves apart from the life of the community, and that the time has come for this policy to change. Not only should the school work closely with parents and involve them in its work; it should welcome youth clubs and evening classes within its walls, and cricket teams on its sacred pitches. Its pupils should be encouraged to serve the old and the needy in the neighbourhood and its staff to join in cultural activities. A close connection between schools and Colleges of Further Education will help to encourage the idea that education does not finish with school-leaving, and, for many, further and adult education will be the way towards continuing development. Many schools appear to know little of this field; each school should have complete programmes of courses in colleges of further education, university departments of Adult Education and the W.E.A. and should make a positive attempt to encourage their pupils to join in. Courses in these colleges might be used by sixth-formers as part of their general studies, and adult education departments could organise courses to take place in schools as they do already in factories and mines. Why, indeed, should there not be an attempt to integrate the top of a grammar school with further and adult education activities? Our education system contains too many air-tight compartments. The grammar school can be just as effective a community school as can the comprehensive school, and has far more to gain than to lose from this.

It must be obvious that much which has been written suggests demands on our teachers that many of them are neither qualified nor even trained to meet. This is no place for detailed discussion of the training of teachers, but certain things might briefly be said. Jean Floud has pointed out that the day of the teacher missionary—spreading cultural light in dark places—has gone and the teacher should now be looked on rather as a social worker, trained to understand the needs of his pupils, the nature of society, and their place in it. A strong sociological bias, an emphasis on the psychology of child development, a concentration on the real problems which arise in school, these will provide a training which the student will recognise as relevant and which can certainly lead to a study of education which is academically respectable. The point is important that the student should recognise the relevance and 'school-centredness' of what he is doing, and one therefore welcomes experiments which involve associating the schools much more closely with teacher-training. Two routes ought to be open, a college-based and a school-based training, perhaps as a start for post-graduate students. The University Education Department which sympathises with the desire of teachers to play a more effective part in training, however, is in somewhat of a dilemma. What will the effect of this be on the student? Will they be encouraged to retain flexibility of mind and the ability to adapt to a changing situation, or is there a danger that some of the worst of existing teaching methods and attitudes may be perpetuated? Underlying all these considerations, however, is a need to produce teachers who possess mature well-balanced personalities able to cope with the more relaxed relationships in schools and the pressures and tensions generated by the developing teenager. Teaching consists of much more than the transmission of information: it is concerned with a communication of standards and values which can only take place if there are effective personal relations between individuals, and it is at this point that the mature personality has to bear the strain.

It must be obvious to all that the world of education is today faced with the appallingly difficult task of cultural integration, if we are to avoid the division of our society into a small cultural élite and a large popular culture. What we have to aim at is a cultural diversity, a spectrum, with a common attachment to common institutions and to a basic democratic way of life. In spite of cries of woe from certain intellectuals, obsessed with the low standard of many of the cultural influences which affect society, there are some favourable tendencies at work. The tremendous increase in car ownership and continental holidays notably extends the range of experience and helps to break down parochial and insular attitudes. The paperback revolution, the spread of better reading habits through public libraries, increased attendance at art galleries, concerts and theatres (especially where there is an exciting new theatre as in Nottingham) are very encouraging signs. Colleges of Further Education, evening institutes and adult education classes show increased membership. There is great enthusiasm for hobbies, crafts, home decoration, gardening, the possession of musical instruments, and a vast development of clubs and societies of all sorts has taken place. Even television itself, to some the root of all evil, is not wholly bad and we know already about the change from an almost drug addiction to a much more selective viewing which gradually stimulates a more creative use of leisure. But perhaps the most interesting and encouraging sign of all is the teenage rebellion against the standards of the adult world. Colin McInnes has described to us a teenage culture which is classless and international, has values of its own which are far removed both from the stifling narrowness of the old working-class life and the dull, stuffy respectability of the middle classes. Young people are gay and almost offensively clean, paying a degree of attention to their appearance and their clothing which their fathers, at least, find unbelievable. They are much more mature than they used to be, have well-developed interests, leisure time occupations and values of their own. They, just as much as adults, are offended by the lawless gangsters and delinquents who are so effectively advertised by the popular Press. It is fascinating to speculate as to the future of these teenagers, and to ask what sort of adults they will grow into and what sort of a grown-up world they will produce.

What must be quite clear is that the schools should ally themselves with the encouraging changes which are taking place. The teenager in the grammar school must continue to feel at one with the other members of his age-group, must retain his roots in his own background, but at the same time must be helped to free himself from its narrowing and restricting tendencies. He can then develop along lines which have meaning for him, whether it be in the field of music, writing, painting, politics, social or international service, science or technology. He must be freed from inarticulateness and the inhibitions which prevent thought and effective self-expression. His school must work with him, not against him, starting with and through science fiction and the Beatles, using the art lesson to develop discrimination in furniture, china, carpets and curtains—after all there can be a fashion for Swedish furniture as well as for Italian clothing. Given the stimulus many young people find it easy to learn to appreciate modern painting, sculpture or music, much easier in fact than their elders. An interest in town planning, the sociological implications of the motor-car, the different ways of housing an expanding population is already there, waiting to be roused into life. The point here is that none of this need be thought of as 'culture' in an oppressive sense; it is part of the stuff of the life of young people, is immediately relevant, and is obviously more attractive than preparation for passing O Level in a conventional subject.

The fact must be faced that few of us live permanently on the cultural heights; few of us read Henry James or listen to Bartok all the time. There are many shared television programmes which influence people throughout society, newspapers which are read, great houses which are visited and football matches which are watched by people with very different educational experiences. Obviously the more shared experiences of this type there are, the less will it be possible to think of a cultural division in society and the nearer we shall approach that cultural spectrum which I have mentioned. On the other hand, we must face the fact that people who go on to higher education will inevitably grow away, to some extent, from those who do not; a whole new range of cultural experiences will be available to them. It would be dishonest to suggest that education in a common school could make much difference here. A common culture, in any far-reaching sense, seems to me neither possible nor desirable. As Bantock has indicated, all people can only share identical cultural experiences if we are content with a low level of response. Agreement about the moral basis of society, by which I mean a genuine and deep tolerance and the acceptance of the uniqueness and value of every individual person, provides a foundation for a cultural diversity. Persons operating in groups of those who think and feel with them can in these circumstances grow and develop freely, and so there will come about a 'plural culture' which can be both tough and stable.

The cultural task of the school is then clear. It must concern itself both with the moral basis on which our society rests and with the nourishing of individual talents and interests. It must throw overboard its lingering pre-occupation with a surface gentility and make itself welcoming to children from all kinds of homes. It must provide an atmosphere in which children can grow as persons. It needs to undertake a rigorous revision of its curriculum and syllabus and escape from the frustrations of external examinations. The school has to remember that it is no longer possible to think of a body of culture which is complete and final; rather it must provide an education which may lead to cultural innovation.

We are living in a period of revolution in the world of education. Is it conceivable that the grammar school will be able to remain immune? If it tries to do so, is it not in danger of being discarded altogether as an institution which has been of great value in the past, but has survived too long? It is my case that the country cannot afford to lose some of the values for which the grammar school stands, but that the schools themselves must recognise the need for substantial change if they wish to survive. Many lively minds in these schools have already come to terms with the second half of the twentieth century though still hampered by external pressures, and have done so with no sacrifice of scholastic integrity and intellectual standards. May I plead with those who lack faith and courage, and adhere timidly to past conventions, to face the fact that the outside world has changed and will continue to do so. A teaching profession worthy of the name—and when we are hearing discussions of professional standards it is sad to note how limited and meanly inadequate they often are—will decide for itself what should be taught and how to teach it; it will be aware of the forces which are affecting society, and in response to these will be willing and able to modify its aims and methods. It is lamentable that teachers' associations should spend so much of their time discussing salaries, representation and the machinery of education; what takes place in the classroom often goes by default. The teacher should be the true educational expert and his abdication could well be described as *trahison des cleres*. One looks for a profession which has the stature to put the interests of the children first and to stand firmly by its right to play the major part in determining what takes place in the school—one which will not tolerate the oppressions of the examination industry, but will reduce it to its proper role of handmaid in the educational process, one which will not be subservient to administrators and local politicians (and here one could refer to the insolence of office). The control of a system of education needs the equal co-operation of many partners, among which the teaching profession should claim an important place.

In my view, then, a reformed grammar school, and it must be insisted that many schools are well on the way towards reform, has still a part to play in the civilising of a mass society. In performing this task it will increasingly be joined by other types of schools which will have to face the same problems. The process of revitalising education is gathering strength and the grammar school should throw its weight behind reform. A really democratic way of life demands equal opportunity for all to obtain that kind of education which will enable their capacities and their personalities to develop to the full: it has no place for a division of society into a superior and an inferior cultural group. The result will not be a common culture but a richly varied plural culture in which men fulfil themselves by pursuing their own view of life. The demand on the teacher and the school is that they should enable men to make choices, to learn discrimination and to continue their growth. May they have the stature and the creative imagination to rise to their opportunities.

M

# Appendix 1

# *Billy's Genius*

A curtain raiser for *A Midsummer Night's Dream*

*By William Bugg*

SCENE: *Family of three.* WIFE, HUSBAND *in collarless shirt and braces, and sixth-form boy. All seated round a table.*

WIFE: Any more tea George?

HUSBAND: Ah! No thanks.

[GEORGE *then moves away from the table to an easy chair. Shortly followed by son. The father flicks through the first few pages, and turns to the back page of a newspaper.*]

BOY: Dad . . . Hey, dad . . . can I have the centre pages, there's an article on Shakespeare.

[*Father hands over centre pages.*]

BOY: We're doing a play you know, dad!

GEORGE: No, I didn't know.

BOY: Oh yes, Shakespeare, of course.

GEORGE: Oh! of course (*sarcastic*).

BOY: You know, I feel rather sorry for you in a way, dad.

GEORGE: Oh yes.

BOY: Yes, having missed all this wonderful . . .

[The BOY's voice dies away leaving a short silence, coming in of recorded voice which are the thoughts of father.]

GEORGE (*thoughts*): Here we go again; the usual twice yearly lecture upon the effect of art and culture on the working classes. A full-blooded thesis given to a father by his own son. Oh yes, I know, Billy boy, if only I could have known what it is to be in contact with what HE meant.

[BOY's *voice comes floating back.*]

170

## Billy's Genius

BOY: . . . John Neville, that fabulous actor at the Notts Playhouse, said that . . .

GEORGE (*thoughts*) . . . John Neville? ah yes, he's the chap we paid four and a tanner a time to see in that Corio. Cori. Coriolanus, yes, he was that damn Tory stamping round the stage saying the working classes had B.O. and mouth odour, still he died in the end. No, he wasn't a bad actor, but yon Billy, you're no John Neville.

[BOY's voice comes back]

GEORGE: Yes, I will have that cuppa now, mother.

[*With much grumbling, he receives his tea.*]

[BOY's *voice starts again.*]

BOY: . . . You see it's all to do with his symbolic four at witchcraft and superstition, it practically hits you . . . (*fades away*).

GEORGE: Oh God, is he still on. Ah well prepare for phase two, a complete psychological breakdown of Hamlet and Othello. And I know how it ends—'(*Mocking the* BOY's *voice*)—and it's on Wednesday night and it'll cost you two and six.'

Half a crown! to see him prancing around the stage in a Toga and up to his eyeballs in make-up. Half a crown! to sit for three hours in a draughty school hall. Half a crown! to sit on a hard misshaped bench they call a seat. Well this year I—AM—NOT—GOING!
—I shall make a firm stand . . . (WIFE's *voice brings him back*).

WIFE: Did you hear that George?

GEORGE: What?

WIFE: Our Bill's in a play—at school.

GEORGE: Oh yes dear, I don't think we'll——

WIFE: Oh! We must come Bill, we love seeing you act, don't we George?

GEORGE: Oh, yes dear, of course.

WIFE: What are you doing?

BOY: A Midsummer Night's Dream by W. Shakespeare.

WIFE: Well, I'll go and wash up but you sit there and tell Dad all about it.

DAD: Haven't you got any homework?

BOY: No dad! I've done it all. Well you see dad it's really three plays, one about some court in Athens . . . one about fairies . . .

GEORGE: Fairies! Fairies! that is all I needed—bleeding Fairies. I have got to sit for two hours on a hard seat, in a draughty hall to see my son acting a fairy. I give up, I surrender. A man writes a play about fairies, and My Son! My own flesh and blood, calls him a Genius. A Midsummer Night's Dream? A bloke would need a warped mind to have a dream like that.

[GEORGE *yawns and the scene fades into the opening of Play.*]

# Appendix 2

# Freedom and Reform in the Sixth

A note on the General Studies Association by its Hon.
Secretary, R. Irvine Smith, Stationers' Company School,
Mayfield Road, Hornsey, N.8.

The debate on the Sixth Form curriculum has raised fundamental questions. It has stimulated criticism of the orthodox "subjects" and their G.C.E. syllabuses; it has asked whether what we
are doing in the schools is relevant to the needs of our pupils; it
has brought into the light some of the obstacles which block improvement. The sight of these obstacles has driven some teachers
to despair of our undirected system, based as it is upon the nineteenth century fallacy that freedom from government control is the
same thing as freedom. Schools are in theory free to determine
their own curricula. In practice this means that the content of education is left to the free play of outside influences far stronger than
the will of any but the most exceptional Headmaster or Head-
mistress. In those other areas of our national life where the law of
the jungle operates, success goes to those who hunt in packs. This
is one of the few lessons that can be learnt from the English political
history which still dominates most schools' history syllabuses. Hence
the Agreement to Broaden the Curriculum, by which a group of like-
minded Heads agreed to limit specialist studies to two-thirds of their
Sixth Form timetable. The consequences of such a move could be
disastrous for a single school, but there is some security in knowing
that 350 others are in the same boat. The A.B.C. gesture was the
signal for a counter-attack by the schools on the mindless forces
which had been distorting their curricula and making their freedom
illusory.

The permanent machinery needed to follow up the success of the

A.B.C. has been provided by the General Studies Association. This developed from an informal study-group set up by some teachers at a conference on the Sixth Form Curriculum run by Mr A. D. C. Peterson in 1960. They felt that one approach to the problem of liberalizing the Sixth Form had been under-rated at the conference —the so-called 'Crowther' approach of using 'minority time', that rump of the timetable, for courses of a general nature designed to repair some of the damage done by excessive specialization. For many teachers this approach presented difficulties, such as making the pupils take the non-specialist work seriously, which led them to favour more radical schemes for a total re-casting of the curriculum. Compared with these schemes General Studies seemed a very poor second-best. It could even be a danger to thorough reform, propping up the existing order with a bogus and ineffective concession. Like charity, it seemed the death of revolution. But the teachers who set up the General Studies Research Group took a more Fabian view. The radical schemes might not succeed. General Studies had at least the advantage of existing, and might be capable of improvement. It might even provide a testing-ground for new ideas and new methods, enabling teachers to clarify their views on what exactly was wrong with the existing three A Level curriculum, and what sort of things could be used to modify or replace it. Far from inhibiting further change, experiments in General Studies could prepare the way for it.

At the end of 1962 the group held a conference and set up a more formal association. Within a year the General Studies Association had grown to include over a thousand teachers and Heads of schools, together with representatives of universities, industry and the professions, parents and others concerned about the quality of Sixth Form education. Members set up study groups to discuss aspects such as the problem of assessing the general education of eighteen-year-olds; subject-panels studied the use of specialist subjects in General Studies, one of these, considering the use of History, submitting an interim report in 1964; research projects were undertaken by several members; an international study-cruise was arranged for the summer of 1964, in which 150 Sixth Formers and their French contemporaries shared a Baltic cruise and a General Studies course under the direction of one of the G.S.A.'s Vice-Presidents, Professor Asa Briggs.

The membership of the G.S.A. cuts across subject boundaries and includes secondary schools of all types. It offers a unique opportunity for cross-fertilization between academic disciplines, and for the exchange of ideas across the internal frontiers that at times tend to break the teaching profession up into tribal units. It makes it possible to trace patterns of similarity and difference among schools which face widely different problems and yet hold surprisingly unanimous views on basic principles.

A detailed study of courses offered by member-schools is under way, and until this is completed it is difficult to feel confident about any generalizations about non-specialist work. The gulf between what appears in a written account of a school's work and the reality behind that account can make nonsense of statistical surveys. It means little to say that a school offers so many periods of, say, Civics, Scientific Method, Modern Literature, or Values in the Modern World. What actually goes on in these courses may vary immeasurably from school to school. On the evidence available so far, it seems that schools try to arrange minority time courses in four main fields —social, scientific, moral and aesthetic; that in their selection of topics within these fields they look for relevance to the modern world, importance, and viability in classroom terms; that in their teaching methods they stress pupil participation, and prefer individual project work and group discussion to formal lecturing.

There seems to be wide agreement about basic objectives, and thinking among teachers has moved a long way from the original concept of General Studies as a sort of culture-pill for busy but illiterate scientists. Aims are defined in broader terms; one member aims 'to stimulate thought about, and interest in, the world in which they live'; another encourages his pupils to 'consider the complexities of their own nature and those of the society in which they live". Aims like these underlie much of the work going on, whether the actual courses are on the United Nations, Underdeveloped Countries, Radioactivity, Microbiology, Sources of Morality, Comparative Religion, The Modern Novel, or Architecture and Design.

There is agreement too, about the need to strike out for the highest possible intellectual level: General Studies must be at least as demanding as Advanced Level work. Some teachers feel they can achieve higher levels with their non-specialists than with their Advanced Level people. In General Studies, after all, the topics are important and interesting, chosen with care for their usefulness in fulfilling defined educational objectives: criteria like this have played no noticeable part in the evolution of G.C.E. syllabuses.

The G.S.A. grew out of widespread dissatisfaction with the conventional curriculum, but its name may be misleading if it suggests that teachers who have developed a successful General Studies course are satisfied. Experience of non-specialist work can make one more critical than ever of specialist syllabuses and the external examinations which all too often are the main determinant of these syllabuses. The movement for syllabus reform is being given powerful support by experiments in General Studies, where attention to principles has not yet become subordinate to the need for high grades in the examination. The question 'Are we meeting the pupils' needs to the best of our ability?' has repercussions throughout the school. The old arguments about rigour and scholarship are being shown up as rationalization of vested interests: work on the problems of modern industrial societies can be as scholarly as a study of the Duke of Newcastle's pocket boroughs and what historians have said about them; 'Death of a Salesman' can be studied with as much rigour as 'The Rivals'. And there can be no doubt which type of material is the more relevant to the young people who are doubling the size of our Sixth Forms every eight years.

But the G.S.A. does not seek to replace the old orthodoxy with a new one, or to search for a Final Solution. It may be asking too much to demand as Plato did that the curriculum should lead society: but it should at least be made to catch up and keep pace with a changing world. The G.S.A. aims to keep discussion and experiment moving, in the search for curricula and methods appropriate to the late twentieth century. The schools must first recover their freedom, then use it. Reform will come from no other direction.

# Appendix 3

# *Curriculum Reform*

THOSE INTERESTED in the reform of the teaching of particular subjects may be glad to have the following addresses:

*Science*

    The Nuffield Foundation (Science Project),
    Nuffield Lodge,
    Regent's Park, London, N.W.1.

    The Association for Science Education,
    52 Bateman Street,
    Cambridge.

*Mathematics*

    The School Mathematics Project,
    The University,
    Southampton.

    The Secretary,
    The Midlands Mathematics Project,
    Harold Cartwright School,
    Solihull, Warwicks.

*English*

    The Secretary,
    The National Association for the Teaching of English,
    197 Henley Road,
    Caversham,
    Reading, Berks.

## Appendix 3

*Modern Languages*

Modern Languages in the Grammar School,
Report of Working Party of Division XII of I.A.H.M.,
Incorporated Association of Headmasters,
29 Gordon Square,
London, W.C.1.

# Bibliography

ARENDT, H. *Between the Past and Future*. Faber, 1961.

ARNOLD, M. *Culture and Anarchy*. C.U.P. 1961 (1869).

BANKS, O. *Parity and Prestige in English Secondary Education.* Routledge and Kegan Paul, 1955.

BANTOCK, G. H. *Freedom and Authority in Education*. Faber, 1952. *Education in an Industrial Society*. Faber, 1963.

BERNSTEIN, B. *British Journal of Sociology*, Vol. II, No. 3, 1960. *Language and Social Class.* *Educational Research*, Vol. 3, No. 3. June, 1961. *Social Structure, Language and Learning.*

BLACKHAM, H. J. *Political Discipline in a Free Society*. Allen and Unwin, 1961.

BRAMELD, T. *Cultural Foundations of Education*, Harper, 1957.

COWELL, F. R. *Culture in Private and Public Life*. Thames and Hudson, 1959.

DAVIS, A. *Social Class and Influences Upon Learning*. Harvard U.P., 1948.

DAVY, C. *Towards a Third Culture*. Faber, 1961.

DE HAAN and HAVIGHURST. *Educating Gifted Children*. University of Chicago Press, 1961.

DEWEY, J. *Human Nature and Conduct*. Allen and Unwin, 1922.

DOBINSON, C. H. *Schooling, 1963-70*. Harrap, 1963.

DOUGLAS, J. W. B. *The Home and the School*. Macgibbon and Kee, 1964.

ELIOT, T. S. *Notes Towards the Definition of Culture*. Faber, 1948.

FLOUD, J. E. (ed.). *Social Class and Educational Opportunity*. Heinemann, 1957.

FURNEAUX, W. D. *The Chosen Few*. Oxford University Press, 1961.

GRAVES, J. *Policy and Progress in Secondary Education, 1902-42.* Nelson, 1943.

GURNER, R. *The Day Boy*. Grant Richards, 1924.

# Bibliography

HALSEY, FLOUD and ANDERSON. *Education, Economy and Society*. Free Press, N.Y., 1961.

HOGGART, R. *The Uses of Literacy*. Chatto and Windus, 1957.

HUGHES, A. G. and E. H. *Education—Some Fundamental Problems*. Longmans, 1960.

HUTCHINS, R. M. *The Conflict in Education in a Democratic Society*. Harper, 1953.

JACKSON, B. and MARSDEN, D. *Education and the Working Class*. Routledge and Kegan Paul, 1962.

JACOBS, N. (ed.). *Culture for the Millions*. Nostrand, 1961.

JEFFREYS, M. V. C. *Beyond Neutrality*. Pitman, 1955.

KROEBER A. L., and KLUCKHOHN, C. *Culture—A Critical Review of Concepts and Definitions*. Harvard University Press. 1952.

LEAVIS, F. R., and THOMPSON, D. *Culture and Environment*. Chatto and Windus, 1933.

LOOMIS, C. P. *Social Systems*. Nostrand, 1960.

MAYS, J. B. *Education and the Urban Child*. University of Liverpool Press, 1962.

NIBLETT, W. R. (ed.) *Moral Education in a Changing Society*. Faber, 1963.

NORDSKOG, J. E. *Social Change*. Morgan Hill, 1960.

OTTAWAY, A. K. C. *Education and Society*. Routledge and Kegan Paul, 1962.

RICHMOND, W. K. *Culture and General Education*. Methuen, 1963.

RUSSELL, B. *Fact and Fiction*. Allen and Unwin, 1961.

SNOW, C. P. *The Two Cultures*. C.U.P. 1959.

STEVENS, F. M. *The Living Tradition*. Hutchinson, 1960.

WARNER, W. L., HAVIGHURST, R. J., and LOBB, M. B. *Who Shall Be Educated?* Kegan Paul, Trench and Trubner, 1946.

WHITEHEAD, A. W. *The Aims of Education*. Benn, 1932.

WILLIAMS, R. *Culture and Society*. Chatto and Windus, 1958.
*The Long Revolution*. Chatto and Windus, 1961.
*Communications*. Pelican, 1962.

WOLHEIM, R. *Socialism and Culture*. Fabian Society, 1961.

## Official Publications

Ministry of Education. Central Advisory Council for Education (England), 15–18, Vol. 1, *Report*.
Vol. 2, *Surveys*. (Chairman: Sir Geoffrey Crowther.) H.M.S.O., 1960.

Board of Education. Secondary School Examinations Council. (Chairman: Sir Cyril Norwood.) H.M.S.O., 1943.

179

# Bibliography

Board of Education. *Report of the Consultative Committee on Secondary Education with Special Reference to Grammar Schools and Technical Schools.* (Chairman: W. Spens.) H.M.S.O., 1938.

Ministry of Education. Central Advisory Council for Education (England). *Early Leaving.* H.M.S.O., 1954.

Committee on Higher Education. *Higher Education Report of the Committee Appointed by the Prime Minister under the Chairmanship of Lord Robbins, 1961-63.* H.M.S.O., 1963.

Ministry of Education. Central Advisory Council for Education (England). *Half our future.* (Chairman: J. H. Newsom.) H.M.S.O., 1963.

*First Report of U.C.C.A., 1961-3.*

# Index

181

# Index

For Product Safety Concerns and Information please contact our EU
representative GPSR@taylorandfrancis.com
Taylor & Francis Verlag GmbH, Kaufingerstraße 24, 80331 München, Germany